This book belongs to

NORTH STAR BOOKS

Indian
Wars *and* Warriors
West

NORTH STAR BOOKS

Indian
Wars *and* Warriors
West

PAUL I. WELLMAN

Illustrated by Lorence Bjorklund

HOUGHTON MIFFLIN COMPANY BOSTON

The Riverside Press Cambridge

973
Wel

Books by
PAUL I. WELLMAN

Novels
Broncho Apache
Jubal Troop
Angel with Spurs
The Bowl of Brass
The Walls of Jericho
The Chain
The Iron Mistress
The Comancheros
The Female
Jericho's Daughters
Ride the Red Earth

Histories
Death on the Prairie
Death in the Desert
republished together as
The Indian Wars of the West
The Trampling Herd
Glory, God and Gold

Reminiscence
Portage Bay

For younger readers
Gold in California
Indian Wars and Warriors (East)
Indian Wars and Warriors (West)

"As long as the rivers shall run and the grass shall grow" the western Indians in their tepees, their earth-covered lodges and their pueblos expected to inhabit their ancient lands and rove their sacred hunting grounds.

But from east of the Mississippi swarmed an ever-increasing horde of white settlers seeking beaver pelts, gold and land. No wonder the two cultures were soon in deadly conflict. Arrows glinted, carbines spoke, wagon trains were surrounded, forts and villages besieged and the blue-coated cavalry were frequently put to the test by war-bonneted tribesmen led by such fearless chiefs as Roman Nose, Sitting Bull and Crazy Horse.

Paul Wellman has sympathy for both sides of this conflict—for white settlers striving to save their wives and children from the scalping knife, as well as for the desperate Indians watching the swift destruction of their beaver and their buffalo. Mr. Wellman teaches us one of the great truths of history, that there is gallantry as well as villainy on both sides of any great struggle.

In this book, and in its companion volume INDIAN WARS AND WARRIORS (EAST), Paul Wellman has written a brilliant and balanced account of one of the longest and most significant wars in world history—the Three Hundred Year War for the North American continent.

Sterling North
General Editor

CONTENTS

To

that wonderful lady, my aunt

M. Alice Isely

with whom, as a young lad, I

saw the West before it was

tamed, and who was never too

busy to help and guide me as

I gained my first deep taste

of its history.

Probable Location of
INDIAN TRIBES
of
WESTERN NORTH AMERICA
Before White Settlement

Beyond the Mighty Mississippi | 1

No SOONER had the young American republic won its freedom and established its claim (still somewhat disputed) to the territories east of the Mississippi, than men began to look across that mighty river to the lands beyond. The Father of Waters, as the Indians called it, was a natural boundary, dividing roughly the eastern third of the continent from the western two-thirds, its length spanning the distance from the Canadian border to the Gulf of Mexico.

West of the river, the territories were claimed by France and Spain, but the claims were weak, since neither nation had populated or developed the country to any great extent. To the enterprising, adventurous Americans, the trans-Mississippi was like a vacuum of wasted lands and resources. Nature abhors a vacuum, and it was inevitable that the tide of population would presently flow over the West.

The fact that the West was more or less occupied by Indian tribes hardly entered into men's consideration. There were wild and spectacular horseback tribes, dwellers in tepees and wearers of war bonnets, like the Sioux, Cheyennes, Blackfeet, Crows, and Comanches; tribes that lived in earth-covered lodges, but roved and warred, like the Pawnees, Arikaras, and Mandans; tribes that dwelt in thatched houses like the Caddos and Wichitas; tribes that built fortifications of stone or adobe, like the Pueblos; tribes that roamed the deserts, like the Paiutes, Navajos, and fierce Apaches; tribes that built large plank houses and raised grotesque totem poles, like the Haidas and Nootkas of the far Pacific Coast.

But, to the white man's mind, these Indians did not use the land. Except for the farming of the Pueblos and a little haphazard gardening by squaws of other tribes, there was no agriculture. Almost all that immense country was no more than a hunting and wandering ground for savage nomads. The American of that day was first of all a farmer, to whom good land fairly cried for the plow, the seed, and the harvest. Secondarily, he was a trader, and an eager searcher for natural resources which could be turned to profit — furs at first, then minerals and timber.

As soon as the Louisiana Purchase of 1803 gave them the right to enter the West, Americans did so. At once they encountered the Indians and almost immediately bloodshed followed. Unhappily, there were some among those who first penetrated the wilderness who were far from admirable. Not a few pioneers hated Indians, because of episodes in the Indian wars still in progress east of the Mississippi. Others were animated by sheer greed.

On the other hand, the warlike tribes did not tamely submit to invasion of their hunting grounds. They fought and killed. Sometimes they were savagely cruel.

There were heroisms and tragedies, atrocities and massacres on both sides. But in every instance the white men were the aggressors. It is not a part of our history upon which we can look back with much pride, but this should be remembered: the white pioneer men and women who dared and suffered greatly were simple people in most instances, seeking only to build homes in what appeared to them an empty land, and cultivate a bit of soil to support themselves and their families. The conscience of the times was very different from ours. And in the final analysis, for all its bloodshed, the conquest of the West was necessary, and has provided its own justi-

fication in the fine cities, happy homes, prosperity, and
peace it made possible.

First came the trappers — the Mountain Men —
fanning out across the great country beyond the
Mississippi, seeking haunts of beaver and other furred
animals, until they knew almost every river, creek,
lake, valley, mountain pass, or desert route in the
entire West.

Already, in 1804, when the young army captains,
Meriwether Lewis and William Clark, began their
great exploration across the continent, following the
Louisiana Purchase, they found trappers and traders
in the Missouri River country before them; and from
then on Americans of wild and adventurous spirit
went everywhere and feared nothing.

George Frederick Ruxton, British army officer and
sportsman, left a description of a typical Mountain
Man:

His body [was] bent over his saddle horn, across which
rested a long and heavy rifle, his keen gray eyes peering
from under the slouched brim of a flexible felt hat, black
and shining with grease. His buckskin hunting shirt,
bedaubed until it had the appearance of polished leather,
hung in folds over his bony carcass . . . He *appeared*
to look neither to the right or left, but in fact his little
twinkling eye was everywhere . . . Acquainted with

every inch of the Far West, and with all the Indian
tribes who inhabited it, he never failed to outwit his red
enemies, and generally made his appearance at the ren-
dezvous with galore of beaver . . . When attacked by
Indians [he] invariably fought manfully, and with all the
coolness that perfect indifference to death or danger would
give . . . His rifle cracked away merrily, and never spoke
in vain; and in a charge — if it came to that — his keen-
edged butcher knife tickled the fleece of many a Blackfoot
. . . His iron frame defied fatigue . . . and, when game
was scarce and they suffered from hunger . . . [he] never
grumbled . . . [but] chewed away at his shoes with
relish even, and as long as he had a pipeful of tobacco
to his pouch was a happy man.

Almost as savage as the Indians themselves — with whom they sometimes traded, sometimes lived, and sometimes fought deadly battles — those nameless wanderers were the real pathfinders who showed later government expeditions the unknown routes across the western continent.

Of laws the Mountain Men knew little and cared less. What they wanted they took, and as a result their constant clashes with the wild tribes made their chances of a long life slim indeed. Among them some became famous, like Kit Carson and Jedediah Smith — men with genuine nobility of character — and also Jim Bridger, Broken Hand Fitzpatrick, Old Bill Williams, and others. But there also were among them scoundrels, like James Johnson and his crew in New Mexico, who murdered Indians to collect scalp bounties, and so lit the fires that burned for generations in the hate of the Apaches.

At the beginning of the last century, Arizona, New Mexico, western Texas, and northern Old Mexico were the roving grounds of the Apaches, a people so fierce that they were named for their one outstanding trait — *apache* is the Papago word for "enemy."

Their principal bands were: the Mimbreños, along the Mimbres River of New Mexico; the Jicarillas, in northern New Mexico; the Mescaleros, in the Davis

Mountain country of Texas; the Tontos, Gilas, Chiricahuas, and White Mountain Apaches of Arizona.

About 1804, Lieutenant Colonel Manuel Carrisco,
a Spanish officer commanding military posts in New
Mexico, discovered a great copper deposit at Santa
Rita del Cobre (now Santa Rita). It was worthless to
him, because it was in the very heart of the country of
the Mimbreños — the fiercest of all the Apaches, who
had been at war with the Mexicans for generations.

He therefore sold his interests to Don Francisco
Manuel Elguea, of Chihuahua, who in 1822 succeeded,
with bribes, in making a treaty whereby the Indians
permitted him to work the mines. For fifteen years
the mining continued, and the copper produced was
so pure that the Mexican government mint contracted
for all of it for coinage.

But though the Apaches did not molest the miners
or the pack trains that carried supplies north from
Chihuahua, and copper south, they by no means considered themselves bound to keep peace with the rest
of Mexico. Continually they raided deep into Sonora
and Chihuahua, leaving dead bodies and burned
dwellings behind, and bringing back horses, plunder,
and captives.

Made desperate by the Apache raids, which the
soldiers seemed powerless to stop, the government of
Chihuahua in 1837 made a new law — a barbarous

law, a last-ditch law, a law conceived by men who could not meet the Apache menace by any civilized means. It was a scalp-bounty law, by which the state offered to pay a sum equal to $100 for the scalp of every Apache warrior brought to the capital; $50 for the scalp of each squaw; and $25 for the scalp of each child. Sonora also made such a law.

It was a peerless chance for the unscrupulous. Until then Apache enmity had been directed at the Mexicans. There were only a few Americans in the country, but among these was James Johnson, who, with two men named Eames and Gleason, led a band of trappers.

With a dreadful greed for gold, Johnson planned

to put scalp-collecting in the realm of big business, by a wholesale slaughter. So he and his crew went to Santa Rita, and enlisted the aid of the soldiers of the *presidio* (fort), and the civilians of the settlement to aid in his scheme.

Not far from the copper mines was a Mimbreño village. These Apaches were invited to a great feast, and all came. Barbecued steers, corn meal mush, and *mescal* (an intoxicating drink made from maguey cactus) were served to them in the plaza. To one side lounged Johnson and his men, near a screening of branches and sacking. What the Indians did not know was that behind that screen squatted the ugly bulk of a cannon, loaded to the muzzle with bullets,

nails, pieces of chain, slugs, and stones, ready to fire.

At the middle of the feast, sacks containing *soccorro* (corn meal) were heaped in the center of the plaza, and the Indians told to help themselves. Laughing and chattering, not dreaming of treachery, the squaws and children gathered about this "gift."

When the crowd was thickest, Johnson touched the lighted end of his cornhusk cigarette to the vent hole of the gun. A shattering blast tore apart the screen and the devil's collection of missiles mowed a dreadful, blood-spattered swath through the Indians.

With that, Mexican soldiers and civilians and American trappers leaped forward, muskets and rifles blazing, to finish the slaughter. In wildest panic the Apaches fled in every direction. Only the swiftest escaped. The ground was heaped with corpses. Johnson and his crew collected what represented, to them, a small fortune in scalps.

In their village, the surviving Mimbreños counted their losses. Scores, chiefly women and children, had been murdered, a disaster the like of which the tribe had never known.

It was a moment of despair and sorrow; but in that moment a chief stepped forward who was to become the greatest Apache leader of all time.

His name was Mangas Coloradas (Spanish for "Red

Sleeves," and usually pronounced as if Mangus Colorado by the whites). Among a people rather below the average in height and size, he was a giant, standing six feet six inches tall. There is no portrait of him, but descriptions say his head was great in proportion, the eyes deep-sunk and very bright, lips wide and thin as a knife slash, and a great eagle's beak of a nose curving down to meet the rocky outjut of his chin.

Some time before he had focused the eyes of the Apaches on himself. He had then two Apache squaws in his lodge, but he captured a Mexican girl and added her to his household — making her an equal with his other women, instead of turning her over to his wives as a slave.

His Apache squaws were insulted, and appealed to their relatives. As a result, Mangas Coloradas was challenged to a duel by a brother of each — naked save for a breechclout, with knives as weapons, and death to the vanquished. In the presence of the whole village he slew both his challengers. Thereafter none questioned his right to do as he chose.

The Apache giant looked over the depleted ranks of his people. Evidently he had studied the warriors with some great crisis in mind, for then, or soon after, he named a group of subchiefs under him, all of whom made themselves names in the wars to follow: Delgadito (the Slender), Poncé, El Chico, Pedro Azul,

Coletto Amarillo (Yellow Tail), Cuchillo Negro (Black Knife), and last but not least, the warrior who was to go down in history as Victorio.

Terribly, Mangas Coloradas and his Apaches repaid Johnson's treachery. On the Gila River, not far from Santa Rita, were two trapping parties, one of twenty-two men led by Charles Kemp, the other of three, headed by Benjamin D. Wilson.

The Kemp party, camped in a deep ravine, was surprised at gray dawn by Mangas. Not one survived the hail of his warriors' bullets and arrows. Wilson and his companions were captured alive by stealth. For some reason Mangas let Wilson go free. The others were tortured to death. Wilson reached Santa Fe in the last stages of exhaustion, but lived to be a noted rancher, a state senator in California, and the first American mayor of Los Angeles.

Next Mangas turned his attention to Santa Rita itself. Invisibly his warriors lay about it, watching day and night, so that none dared set foot outside. Meantime he cut off supply trains, ambushing them in the mountains, killing all with them, and taking for his tribe their food and munitions.

One such caravan was destroyed at the foot of the Organ Mountains. Later the dead bodies of its escort and wagon crews were found and buried, each with

a wooden cross on its grave. So many of these crosses were there, that the place became known as Las Cruces (The Crosses). The present town of Las Cruces, New Mexico, stands on the site of this massacre.

Slowly Santa Rita starved. The people watched, at first hopefully, then despairingly, for the supply trains that never came. When it was evident that no help would ever come, it was decided that the whole population, some 300 or 400 men, women, and children, must attempt the long, hazardous, heat-smitten, and all but waterless journey, to the military post of Janos, the nearest refuge to the south, in Chihuahua.

But in so doing they had to run the gantlet of Apaches. In one narrow mountain canyon after another arrows whizzed and rifle bullets sang from the cliffs above, while the refugees died as they struggled on. Harried, pursued, never permitted to rest, the pathetic caravan was almost wiped out. A bare remnant — one authority says only four or five — at last reached Janos. The bleaching skeletons of the rest sprawled behind along that terrible trail.

And what of Johnson, the man who loosed this hell's broth of wrath? Before the final flight from Santa Fe, he and his men attempted to escape, but were driven back by the Apaches. The Indians never were able to account for Johnson, the man they hated most. Did he win free? It is hardly likely, for he was

not again heard about, and no record can be found
that he ever collected the bounty from the government of Chihuahua for the scalps reaped by his
treachery. One story, which seems believable, is that
he died in Santa Rita of smallpox, which broke out
in the village before the evacuation. Whatever his
fate, it was deserved.

Meantime, the Mimbreños feasted and rejoiced
over the purging of their country of Mexicans and
white men. Yet even then a greater shadow was
gathering. In 1836 — about two years before the
final downfall of Santa Rita — Texas rebelled against
Mexico and won independence. It would soon be
annexed by the United States, and war was brewing
with Mexico.

The Apaches had best get ready, for that war was
destined in a brief span of years to bring into their
country something far greater than anything they had
thus far faced. This time it would be no single mining
village to combat, but an irresistible migration of a
virile, aggressive people, who could, if necessary, be
as fierce and deadly as the Apaches themselves — the
Americans.

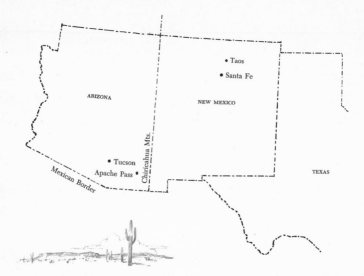

The Grievance of Mangas Coloradas | 2

THE NAME Mangas Coloradas is perhaps not as well known to modern readers as the names of some later chiefs, such as Cochise, Geronimo, and others — simply because these came later and hence received more publicity. But the giant Mimbreño was undoubtedly the greatest Apache of history. In his time Cochise and Geronimo, and the others, were proud to serve as his lieutenants. He, for once, knit the Apache peoples together, and made the Southwest almost a void as far as white men were concerned.

Yet even after his experience at Santa Rita, Mangas at first tried to conciliate the Americans. It was only when he suffered a piece of stupid cruelty at their hands that he went to war forever against them.

When the Mexican War began in 1846, an American army under General Stephen W. Kearny captured Santa Fe and other New Mexico towns, and the province was proclaimed United States territory. There was one brief outbreak by the Indians of Taos Pueblo, which was quickly put down; but by then Kearny already was marching toward California. As he did so, Apache scouts paralleled every foot of his way.

He camped at Santa Rita, and there was met by Mangas and several of his subchiefs. The Apaches highly approved of his war against their enemies, the Mexicans, and offered to help, but were refused. Kearny moved on, to take possession of California, and thus the first American invasion of Apache country ended without bloodshed.

But in February, 1848, gold was discovered in California. Shortly after, that strange stampede known as the California Gold Rush began. Desperately the wagon trains pushed westward, thrusting out of their way Indians who inhabited the country, deaf to anything but their desire for gold — gold — gold.

Inevitably the Indians fought back, both along the Overland Trail in the north, and the Gila River Route in the south. For some time, however, the Mimbreño country was not directly affected. Then, in 1851, a boundary commission, with a heavy military escort, under J. R. Bartlett, began to survey the newly defined

Mexico–United States border. When it camped near the ruins of Santa Rita, Mangas Coloradas himself called on Bartlett, to ask if he meant to stay. Assured that the surveying commission would soon be on its way, the chief departed to his own camp.

But soon disputes arose. The white men released two Mexican boys who were captives of the Indians, which brought a protest. A little later a Mexican laborer named Lopez killed an Apache during a petty argument.

Bartlett put Lopez under arrest. Very soon a deputation of Apache chiefs came, demanding that the Mexican be surrendered to them. Bartlett, a just man, explained that he could not do so, but promised that the man would be tried in Santa Fe, and if found guilty, hanged.

"The Apaches will not be satisfied to *hear* that the murderer has been punished in Santa Fe," said the chiefs. "They want to *see* him punished here — where all the Apaches can see him put to death."

Bartlett offered to keep the murderer in chains and make him work, giving the money he earned to the family of the slain man.

"Money will not satisfy an Apache for the blood of a brave!" exclaimed the chiefs with scorn. They departed.

Horses and mules began to disappear from the commission's herd. When Bartlett moved on, he had lost nearly 200 animals, and his command was almost on foot. The Apaches, of course, believed they had driven him away.

Meantime, while the commission was at Santa Fe, someone discovered gold in the nearby Piños Altos Mountains. A number of miners assembled there, and they remained after Bartlett had gone on.

To Mangas they were a source of keen anxiety. He studied them, and was puzzled to find that they toiled among the sizzling rocks for nothing more important or usable (to him) than the yellow metal known to the Mexicans as *oro* — gold. Perhaps, if he could show the white men where they could find more *oro* than at Piños Altos, they might leave his country!

After a time he came to them, saying he knew where much more *oro* could be found. Probably he told the truth, for there was a great deal of gold in the area. But the miners could think only of treachery.

One of them, perhaps drunk, suggested that they tie up the chief and whip him. The idea was accepted. A dozen men leaped on Mangas Coloradas, and in spite of his great strength, bore him down. Rawhide cords were lashed about his wrists and he was spread-eagled on a tree.

There is no record that he winced or uttered a sound in the lashing with a blacksnake whip that followed.

An Apache knew how to bear agony.

At last they released him, and jeered him out of camp. It would have been better for the whole white population of the Southwest if they had finished by killing him. For Mangas never forgot the whipping. It was the worst insult an Indian could receive, and he devoted the rest of his life to avenging that pain and shame.

At once he began to raid, harrying settlements in New Mexico and Arizona, cutting off wagon trains, even going out into the plains of Texas in search of ease for his scarred back. Never had the Apaches seen a chief so single-purposed in destruction. It was the beginning of a war that in half a century of time cost thousands of lives and millions of dollars. The total number of white men who died quickly in the heat of a rush or by ambush, or slowly under Apache torment, will never be known.

Among all the chiefs of other Apache bands, Cochise, the snake-like Chiricahua, was the nearest to Mangas' heart. To him the Mimbreño gave his comeliest daughter as wife, and often the two met and smoked in friendship. Yet, though Cochise willingly warred on Mexicans, he held back from fighting Americans — until a happening in 1860, which made a changed man of him.

Cochise

That October a raiding party of Apaches drove off a herd of cattle belonging to Johnny Ward, a rancher on the Sonoita River, in Arizona. They also carried off a child, half Indian, whose mother, a Mexican woman, lived on the ranch.

Bugles sang in Fort Buchanan (about twenty-five miles east of Tubac, Arizona) and sixty men under a greenhorn young officer, Second Lieutenant George W. Bascom, rode out to search for the stock and child. Bascom knew of one Apache camp — near a spring in Apache Pass, a deep and narrow cut in the Chiricahua Mountains, through which went the Butterfield stage route.

It happened to be Cochise's camp of Chiricahuas,

near the stone stage station, kept by a man named Wallace, who bought wood from the Indians. The friendliness of Cochise is shown by the fact that the stage line was operating without trouble through the heart of the Chiricahua country.

To this place Bascom led his men, and invited Cochise and several of his warriors to confer with him. He accused the Chiricahuas of taking the cattle and the child and demanded their return. Cochise replied that he did not have them and knew nothing of the raid, but offered to find out what band was responsible for it, and tell the officer.

Bascom lost his head. Though the Indians had come into his camp on a friendly invitation, he ordered them arrested and placed in a tent under guard.

Arrest Cochise? Not while he could fight!

He drew a knife from his breach clout, slashed open the rear of the tent, and with a war whoop like an eagle's scream leaped for freedom, followed by his warriors. Right through the soldier ranks the Apaches charged. All but five escaped. Cochise was wounded by a bullet in his flight.

At once Bascom found himself and his men fighting for their lives, with Apaches shooting at them from the canyon walls all about them. In one act he had changed a peaceful Apache band into murderous enemies.

By nightfall several men were wounded, while the Indian fire continued heavy from the canyon walls. In the darkness a daring trooper managed to slip through the cordon, reaching Fort Buchanan. Captain B. J. D. Irwin, with a detachment, rode to Bascom's relief, capturing a lone Indian on the way.

Meantime the Apaches attacked a wagon train coming up the pass, killed eight men, and took captive three more. These, with three other white prisoners — including Wallace, the station agent — Cochise offered to exchange for the six captured braves. Bascom refused.

Now two more companies of troops arrived, and the Apaches withdrew into the mountains. As the soldiers retired from the pass with their wounded, they found the six white prisoners, who had been tortured to death and left for the buzzards. They hung the Indian prisoners at the same spot, for Cochise to cut down.

In two days the treachery to Cochise had cost 20 white and 8 Indian lives. But the total cost was far graver than that. From then on the Chiricahuas never really ceased war for a quarter of a century.

Mangas Coloradas had an eager ally at last. With Cochise he all but depopulated southern New Mexico and Arizona. Settlements in the Santa Cruz and Gila valleys were desolated. All ranches were destroyed. Tubac was deserted, never to become a flourishing town again. Tucson dwindled to a village of 200 souls, in constant terror of an Apache attack.

With the beginning of the Civil War in 1861, the Confederates found themselves as much involved as the Union with the Apaches, who made no distinction between blue and gray uniforms, as long as the wearers were white men.

Mimbreños and Mescaleros devastated the Big Bend country of Texas. Settlers deserted it, marching troops were ambushed, and when the Confederate forces withdrew from it, the Apaches sacked and burned Fort Davis.

With 200 warriors, Mangas Coloradas swooped

down on his old enemies at the Piños Altos mines, but the arrival of cavalry saved them — to his bitter disappointment, since this touched his deepest hate.

In July, 1862, word came from Cochise, who was watching in the Chiricahua Mountains, of a great army marching from the west. It proved to be the California Brigade, under General J. H. Carleton, heading east to join the Union forces in New Mexico. Mangas went to see, and with his friend watched the towering dust cloud approaching Apache Pass. The two chiefs decided to fight the white men there.

Just before the battle, Mangas evened his score with Piños Altos. Fourteen of the miners had started west, perhaps to meet Carleton. Noting their direction, the

chief prepared a net for them. Two miles from the eastern buttresses of the mountains ran a rugged gully which could not be seen unless one came right upon it. There he placed his warriors.

On came the Piños Altos men. Suddenly the earth seemed to open up before them. Half of them were downed by the first volley; the rest died in the swooping rush that followed. The fourteen bodies, pincushioned with arrows, were found days later by a detachment of soldiers under Captain John C. Cremony.

Now Mangas Coloradas prepared to meet the oncoming soldiers from California. The advance guard — three companies of infantry, a troop of cavalry, and two howitzers, under Captain Thomas Roberts — entered the pass, with no thought of danger. Halfway up, the dread Apache yell echoed from wall to wall of the gorge, and bullets and arrows rained on the troops.

Back tumbled the soldiers out of the canyon, with triumphant Apache whoops following them. But there were springs up the pass, and no other water was available. Roberts had to reach them.

He brought up his artillery. For the first time the Apaches faced big guns, which they said "shot twice" — for the shells exploded when they struck. The Indians retreated and Roberts reached the springs.

That evening he sent back a messenger with an

escort to warn Captain Cremony, who was following with a pack train, and to ask for reinforcements, since he expected a harder fight next day. But in the morning, when his soldiers expected a full-scale attack by the Apaches, nothing happened. A few Indians were seen in the heights, but these disappeared, and Roberts, hardly believing his luck, marched on through in safety.

What happened between night and morning to change the Apaches from dangerous resisting warriors to fugitives? It is a tale of a strange turn of fortune, coupled with the courage of one man.

The message escort sent by Roberts to Cremony was pursued almost at once by mounted Apaches. In the running fight that followed, two or three men were wounded. Then the horse of Private John Teal was killed. The soldier found himself on foot in the midst of his enemies, for his comrades, who were riding for their own lives, could not help him.

Teal had no hope of escaping. He only wanted to sell his life as dearly as he could. Crouching behind his dead horse, he began firing with his carbine at the Indians, who were galloping about, preparing to charge down upon him.

Their leader, he noticed, was a giant. If he only could bring down that chief!

He held his breath as he aimed, and when the

sights of his carbine caught the broad brown chest, he pulled the trigger. Down, crashing out of the saddle, fell the huge warrior!

Darkness was now falling. To Teal's astonishment the Apaches seemed at once to lose all interest in him. He could hear their exclamations as they gathered about the fallen chief, and then "their voices growing fainter in the distance." For a time he waited. Then he rose and walked eight miles back to Cremony — carrying his saddle and bridle, for he was of a thrifty nature. Not an Indian did he see on the way.

No wonder. Teal did not dream whom he had hit, but it was Mangas Coloradas himself who was felled by his bullet.

The Indians left Apache Pass to Carleton's men and bore their leader with wonderful speed and care southward across the mountains into Mexico. Right into the town of Janos they carried him, paying no attention to the soldiers in the *presidio,* who did not venture to come out. Dark warriors occupied the streets while Mexican women and children cowered and prayed behind closed doors. A Mexican doctor was shown the great, limp body of the chief.

"Make him well," said the Apaches. "If he does not die, everybody will live. If he dies, everybody in Janos will die, too."

No physician ever worked with more fearful care than that doctor, knowing that upon his skill depended not only his patient's life, but his own life, and the lives of all the people of Janos. Fortunately the rawhide constitution of the sufferer was in his favor. Mangas Coloradas eventually went back to his mountains.

But the sands were running out for the great Apache. He was now more than seventy years old, and he never fully recovered from his wound. In his age and sickness he began to yearn for peace, and so became an easy victim for a trap set by Captain E. D. Shirland, commanding a company of soldiers, and Joseph Miller, who led a party of prospectors. They sent to him word that they wanted to talk with him — about peace.

Alone, Mangas Coloradas walked into Shirland's camp, January 7, 1863, hoping to discuss a treaty. Instead, he was surrounded and made prisoner.

He knew then that his end had come. Colonel J. R. West, of Fort McLean, rode to the camp when he heard of the capture, arriving after dark. The night was cold and West found Mangas Coloradas wrapped in a blanket beside a big fire. The colonel inspected the two guards, Privates James Collyer and George Mead, to see that their bayonets were fixed. Then he gave them final instructions.

"Men," he growled, "that old murderer has got away from every soldier command and has left a trail of blood five hundred miles on the old stage line. I want him dead or alive tomorrow morning; do you understand? *I want him dead!*"

He tramped away. The soldiers understood. One of them began heating his bayonet in the fire. When it was red hot he plunged it suddenly into the prisoner's leg.

Mangas Coloradas leaped up at the pain. Both guards' rifles rang out together. The Apache fell in a sprawling heap. Collyer and Mead came closer and emptied their revolvers into him.

Mangas Coloradas

The death of Mangas Coloradas was reported by Colonel West as occurring "while trying to get away."

Captain John C. Cremony, who met the chief often, beginning with the Bartlett survey where he was in the escort, and was later agent for the Apaches and knew Mangas Coloradas better than any other white man, left this estimate of him:

He was the greatest and most talented Apache of the 19th Century . . . His sagacious counsels partook more of the character of wide and enlarged statesmanship than those of any other Indian of modern times . . . He found means to collect and keep together, for weeks at a time, large bodies of savages, such as none of his predecessors could assemble and feed . . . and taught them to

comprehend the value of unity and collective strength
. . . Take him all in all, he exercised influence never
equaled by any savage of our time.

The killing of Mangas Coloradas only spurred the
Apaches to greater activity. But for a time the center
of attention on the frontier was focused in a different
direction, by events nearer and more perilous to the
settlements.

Far to the north of the Apache country, in Minnesota, another great Indian war had broken out even
before Mangas' death. The cause was familiar: the
taking of land by too aggressive white men, broken
promises, and realization by the Indians that they had
been cheated. But the warriors were of another tribe
— the mighty Sioux.

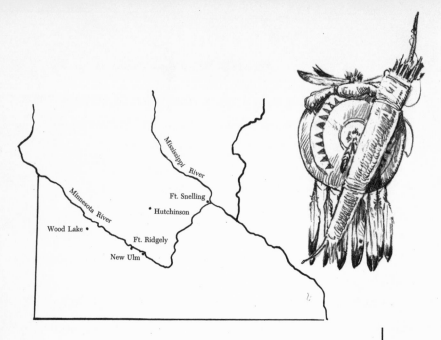

ON SUNDAY MORNING, August 17, 1862, a tall Indian dressed like a white man in neat black broadcloth, but with moccasined feet and his hair in two gleaming black braids, attended services in the Episcopal mission church — of which he was a member — at the Lower Sioux Agency, near Fort Ridgely, Minnesota.

Everyone present knew him: Little Crow, the most important Sioux chief in Minnesota. But nobody knows why he chose to attend church that particular Sunday. Perhaps it was to cloak the already ordered movements of his people, which were to climax in a terrible massacre of the white people. Or perhaps the chief attended the service as a silent farewell to the white men, some of whom had been his friends.

Little Crow was capable of such sentiment. He was an unusual Indian, nearly sixty years old at the time; his manners were those of a refined gentleman, and his ability as an orator and diplomat marked. Sixteen years before, after a drunken fight with his own brother, he nursed a wrist crippled by a bullet, and swore to banish firewater from his tribe. He it was who sent for a Christian missionary "to teach the people the white man's way."

The missionary — Reverend Thomas S. Williamson — came, and the good man won the chief's heart, and those of many of his people. But now that was all forgotten in the grievances of the Sioux, which Little Crow could array in his mind that Sunday morning. His people had been induced to cede most of their fine hunting grounds in 1851, and now were herded on small reservations. Rascally traders used government red tape to withhold food issues from the starving Indians, so that they could sell them wormy flour and spoiled bacon at high prices. Indian women were seduced by evil white men, and half-breed children multiplied, a shame to every honorable Sioux.

The final insult had been given only a week before, when Andrew J. Myrick, a trader, listening to the chiefs pleading for the long promised stores, sneered, "If they're hungry, let them eat grass, for all I care."

The Sioux remembered that. Mentally and physically they were among the finest of all American Indians. Early travelers paid tribute to their courage, skill with weapons, horsemanship, and honor. They were fighters, too. They called themselves Dakota (or Lakota, depending on the dialect), meaning "Allies." But their common name, Sioux, was a shortening of a Chippewa word, *Nadowessioux* (as spelled by the French), meaning "Snakes," and hence "enemies," which they always were to that powerful lake tribe.

As early as 1640 the French knew them. In the Pontiac War they befriended the white men by forbidding the Menominees to attack them; and in the War of 1812, though most of them sided with the British, the

Typical Sioux

Typical Sioux

diplomacy of Manuel Lisa, a St. Louis fur trader, kept them from hostilities.

They were far-spread. Their western division, known as Tetons, lived out on the great buffalo plains. Their eastern divisions, the Santees and Yanktons, dwelled in the woodland country west of Lake Superior. It was these, chiefly the Santees, who looked to Little Crow for leadership.

After service that Sunday morning, the chief greeted with perfect courtesy the white men and women assembled, complimented the minister on his sermon, shook hands with everyone, and rode off — never to return.

Forty miles from the agency, a German farmer, with his wife and daughter, and three guests, sat at Sunday dinner. Suddenly four Indians entered the cabin, rifles crashed, knives flurried, and the happy dinner party lay dead. The Indians rode into the forest.

It was the signal. Up and down the Minnesota River stealthy bands of warriors set forth.

At sunrise, Monday morning, the people at the Lower Sioux Agency were awakened by a gunshot, followed by a hideous war whoop. Rushing out of their doors, they were shot down by the Sioux. The traders were the victims most wanted. Myrick, whose cruel taunt had stirred the hatred of the Indians, was killed in front of his store, and his mouth was stuffed full of grass. Eight other traders met ends as bloody. Only a few white people escaped to Fort Ridgely, fifteen miles downriver, through the heroic efforts of Henry Millier, who plied the ferry across the Minnesota River until he was slain.

Meantime Sioux war parties swept through other settlements. And here occurred what happened so often in Indian wars, and increased the bitterness between red and white men. The people who suffered most were innocent of harming the Indians, except in so far as they had taken up land permitted by the government, under treaty with the Sioux. They were chiefly farm families, many of German or Scandinavian origin, honest, hard-working, and kindly.

But the hatred of the Sioux extended to all white people, without any exceptions, because of the bad deeds of a few. The war parties took the farms as they came, slaughtering the men, carrying off the young women as captives, butchering the children or allowing them to follow their mothers according to the whim of the moment. There were many barbarities. Lake Shetek and Renville County were especially bloody. In the first day more than 200 persons were killed about the Lower Agency. How anyone escaped is a wonder, and there were incidents of great bravery.

Here is one. John Eastlick, with his wife and five boys, lived at the Lake Shetek settlement. When it was overwhelmed, Eastlick and three of the boys were murdered, and Mrs. Eastlick carried off. Before the Indians took her, however, she managed to hide two of her children: her baby, Johnny, and the one surviving older boy, eleven-year-old Merton, whom she charged never to leave his baby brother as long as he lived.

Eventually Mrs. Eastlick managed to escape from the Indians, and was found by August Garzine, a mail carrier, almost crazed by the belief that her whole family was dead. He took her to New Ulm. On the way, forty miles from the massacre, they found Merton and Johnny!

The lad had carried the baby every foot of that dis-

tance, hiding from the Indians and living on berries he managed to find. He was almost as thin as a skeleton, the flesh was worn from his bare feet, and it was days before he was able to speak. But the baby was safe and sound.

How many lost their lives in the great massacre will never be known accurately. Officially recorded, as definitely known, are 644. Hundreds, mostly women, were taken captive. At the end of the war, 269 of these were recovered at one time, and others were rescued later. But the total of men, women, and children who disappeared, never to be heard from again, will never be complete.

As the first haggard refugees from the Lower Agency burst into Fort Ridgely with their fearful story, Captain John S. Marsh sent a rider to Fort Snelling, asking help, and with forty-six men marched for the Agency.

On the way the soldiers met streams of fugitives, heard hysterical tales, and passed dead bodies, which told them they were in the midst of a great disaster — an Indian uprising of nightmare proportions. But when they reached the ferry, which crossed the Minnesota River to the Agency, nobody was in sight, though the buildings across the stream were in flames.

Had the Indians left? No, at that very moment 200 Sioux warriors, with rifles cocked, lay hidden in the trees and bushes near at hand and on the same side of the river. An Indian, recognized as White Dog, a subchief, walked from among the burning buildings and motioned the soldiers across.

Marsh hesitated. All at once the smoke and reports of guns burst from scores of hiding places. Half a dozen soldiers were killed at the first volley. Marsh tried to charge the Indians ambushed on his flank, saw it was useless, and ordered a retreat.

Pursued by the Sioux, the captain attempted to lead his men across the river, and was drowned in the eddies of the swift current. Exactly half the command, including the captain, were dead when the survivors reached the fort late that evening.

Fort Ridgely that night was a scene of terror. Frightened women begged their friends to shoot them rather than let the Indians get them. Lieutenant Thomas P. Gere, now commanding, had only a handful of men. Had the Sioux attacked then, they must have carried the fort and killed all in it.

But though there were a dozen alarms, no Indians appeared. It was later learned that Little Crow could not get his warriors to stop looting long enough to gather for an assault. Next day Lieutenant Timothy J. Sheehan arrived with reinforcements. Including some resolute civilians among the 250 refugees in the fort, he could muster now about 180 men under arms.

The morning of August 20, Little Crow, mounted on a splendid horse, rode up from the west and asked for a parley. It was a ruse to divert attention from the opposite direction, where his warriors were stealing forward.

A burst of firing and wild yells from the east signaled the attack, and the chief rode for cover. So fierce was the Sioux charge that the first line of the fort's defenses was carried. Before the flashing tomahawks, the soldiers, mostly raw recruits, fell back. Desperately, Sheehan tried to rally them on the parade ground, but the Indians, shooting from barracks they occupied, brought some of the men down. The undisciplined troops wavered.

With wild whooping the Sioux issued forth, forming for another charge. Sheehan's men began to retreat; the women watching from the south buildings, where they had been placed, screamed in terror.

And then, at a moment when all seemed lost, unexpected help came.

Fort Ridgely had once been an artillery post, and a few old rusted cannon of various calibers still were parked there. Among the few veteran soldiers in the garrison was a Sergeant Jones, an artilleryman. To vary the monotony of garrison life, Jones drilled a few infantrymen — who took it up for fun — in gunnery practice.

At the first Sioux onset, the old artilleryman thought of his ancient cannon and his amateur gunners. It took a little time to get the guns ready, for the men were, after all, only infantrymen. But just as Sheehan's line on the parade ground broke, the "battery" was in line.

"Aim in their center and fire as rapidly as possible!" shouted Jones.

Across the parade ground the ancient cannons spoke with thundering booms, and a misfit collection of missiles — anything Jones could ram into their muzzles — swept into the Indian ranks. Working like mad, the sergeant and his men rammed home a second round, and once more the rusty fieldpieces roared.

It was too much for the Sioux. They had faced musket fire right bravely, but the "wagon guns" terrified them. At the third discharge they fled, followed by the wild cheering of the soldiers.

Fort Ridgely was saved. Sergeant Jones was a hero in the dispatches. As for the modest old soldier himself, in his terse report he only stated that his amateur gunners and rusty cannon "gave much satisfaction . . . to all who witnessed the action."

New Ulm, a few miles downriver from Fort Ridgely, shared the unhappy distinction of being a point of greatest danger. Into it poured hundreds of refugees,

and a skirmish with the Indians, the morning after the Agency massacre, threw the town into terror of an attack.

Then, early Saturday, August 23, the smoke of burning buildings up the river showed that the Sioux were on their way. In New Ulm there was not one soldier. Judge Charles E. Flandrau, of the state supreme court, had gathered about 250 armed men, all civilians, and these he formed on the prairie half a mile west of the town, to halt the Indians.

On came the Sioux — at least 500 of them — to the attack. With the yelling and shooting, the white men fell back.

Wrote Judge Flandrau later:

White men fight under a great disadvantage the first time they engage [the Indians]. There is something so fiendish in their yells and terrifying in their appearance when in battle that it takes a good deal of time to overcome the sensation it inspires.

Back into the town retreated the civilians, followed by the savages, who set fire to some of the houses and blazed at the defenders from the shelters of evacuated homes. Flandrau rode wildly up the hill, and succeeded in rallying his men.

When Little Crow formed his warriors for a second assault, a withering fire stopped them. Then Flandrau led a furious countercharge, and the Indians were driven out of the town and into the woods beyond.

That night New Ulm stood guard, but Little Crow withdrew. The possibility that the Sioux might drive the settlers out of eastern Minnesota was ended.

The Indian leader, however, was not discouraged. He still held the western part of the state. For the present, the Sioux were content to count scalps and prisoners and gloat over their booty. Though repulsed, their success exceeded their fondest dreams. At one swoop they had won back — so they believed — most of their richest hunting grounds.

Colonel Henry H. Sibley, a stern old soldier with wide knowledge of Indian ways, took command in Minnesota. Three days after the first massacre, he reached the frontier. In four more he had enlisted 1400 men, raw and ill equipped, but the best he could get. Then he marched for Fort Ridgely, keeping his fatigue details busy burying the bodies of murdered settlers, and arrived at that place August 28.

Next day he advanced to the Lower Agency, burying Marsh's soldiers and more than twenty civilians. Thus far not an Indian had been seen, so Major J. R. Brown was sent on west with 200 men, looking for bodies and burying the dead. On the night of September 1, he camped at Birch Coulee.

Little Crow was not asleep. In the dark his braves closed about the camp, and at dawn a volley swept through it, littering the ground with dead and dying men, and stricken horses. Brown's men fought from behind the wagons, but the Indian fire was so heavy that it seemed certain they would all be wiped out.

Sibley, however, heard the distant firing and hurried to the rescue. He arrived in the nick of time. The Indians withdrew, but Brown's camp was a shambles, with 24 dead and 67 wounded — nearly half his command. Sibley retreated to the Agency with the wounded, and the Sioux had won a victory to make up for their defeats at Fort Ridgely and New Ulm.

For two weeks, while Little Crow kept all Minnesota in an uproar, Sibley grimly drilled his recruits. Then, on September 18, he marched up the Minnesota River again, toward the Yellow Medicine River, where he heard the Indians were camped.

Near the mouth of the Yellow Medicine lies Wood Lake. As Sibley's advance passed that pretty body of water and entered the wooded canyon of the Yellow Medicine, rapid reports of rifles sounded. The woods ahead of Major Welsh's command were full of hostiles, who could not be seen. Puffs of smoke, the clatter of shots, a constant piping of bullets, with the occasional smack as one found its mark, were all the men had to go on.

After a halfhearted charge, stopped by the thick undergrowth, Welsh halted, baffled. His men continued to fall about him. At last he retreated toward Sibley's main command, carrying his wounded.

At once the Sioux leaped in pursuit, and for a time there was hand-to-hand fighting. But Sibley sent five companies to Welsh's aid, and the savages were beaten back.

Thereafter, for two hours the Sioux tried bravely but vainly to drive Sibley from the hill where he had formed his men. Once a headlong charge of painted, screaming warriors on the extreme left came near carrying home. But it was finally repulsed. Shells from Sibley's two cannon decided the battle. The Sioux sullenly retired, while Sibley, hampered by his wounded, camped.

By no means was the Battle of Wood Lake a decisive victory. Sibley held his ground, and that was about all that could be said for it. Yet its results were decisive. A good many Indians had been killed, and they grew discouraged. Fall had come, the men must hunt for winter meat, and Little Crow could no longer keep his people together. Soon the great camp on the Yellow Medicine broke up, and the Sioux, in small bands, scattered.

By friendly Indians Sibley sent messages offering pardon to the Sioux not guilty of atrocities, if they would release their prisoners. On the afternoon of September 26, captive women and children numbering 269 were delivered. All wore Indian clothing. Most of them wept with joy and relief. But some merely gave vacant stares. The scenes and experiences through which they had passed had left them dazed and numb. They were sent to Fort Ridgely, and their relatives, if any were left living, claimed them.

The Sioux were beaten in Minnesota. Sibley rounded up 1500 of them in prisons at Fort Snelling and Mankato, but the rest fled far and wide, carrying the seeds of hate to their kindred out on the plains.

Of the Indian prisoners, 392 charged with extreme barbarity, were tried. Only 59 were acquitted, while 307 were sentenced to death and 16 to prison. President Lincoln commuted the sentences of all but 39 whose cruelties were too clearly proved, and all of these were executed, December 28, on a special gallows built for the occasion.

But Little Crow was still at large. Every day there were fresh rumors that he was gathering strength for a new onslaught. So feared was he that settlers refused to return to their homes.

Next summer, July 3, 1863, Nathan Lampson and his son Chauncey were deer hunting in the bush near

Hutchinson, Minnesota, when they surprised two Indians picking berries. Hostile Sioux were still in the country and the elder Lampson fired, wounding one Indian. The other tried to help him onto a horse. As the wounded Indian attempted to fire at his father, Chauncey Lampson shot him dead. The other mounted and escaped. The Lampsons scalped the dead Indian, carted the body to Hutchinson to display it, and then it was buried.

Somewhat later a small band of Indians was captured on Devil's Lake, among them a sixteen-year-old boy. He said his name was Wo-wi-nap-sa, and he was a son of Little Crow. He then made a statement, of which the following is a part:

Father [Little Crow] hid after the soldiers beat us last fall. He told me he could not fight against the white men, but would go below and steal horses from them . . . and then he would go away off. Father . . . wanted me to go with him and carry his bundles . . . There were no horses . . . We were hungry . . . Father and I were picking red berries near Scattered Lake . . . It was near night. He was hit the first time in the side, just above the hip . . . He was shot the second time . . . in the side, near the shoulder. This was the shot that killed him. He told me he was killed and asked for water . . . He died immediately after.

When Sibley read the statement he at once believed that the Indian killed by the Lampsons was Little Crow. The body was taken up, and a deformity in the right wrist, caused by a gunshot wound received in a family feud, gave positive identification.

So died Little Crow, at the height of his power the most feared red man in America, and a scholar and gentleman in his way. Reduced to stripping red berries to sustain life, he was shot by wandering hunters.

But he left a legacy of distrust and hate with his people, which his white foes would encounter farther west, and very soon. For already the Sioux of the plains had clashed with the soldiers, and a great issue was arising which would send them to war — a war in which Little Crow's warriors, who had gone west, would furnish added grounds for bitterness, and play their part in the fighting.

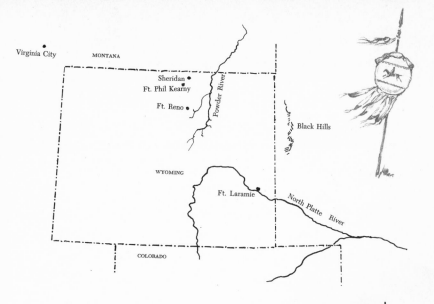

Virginia City

MONTANA

Sheridan •
Ft. Phil Kearny

Ft. Reno •

Powder River

Black Hills

WYOMING

Ft. Laramie

North Platte River

COLORADO

Red Cloud and Fort Phil Kearny | 4

WHILE THE woodland Sioux were fighting in Minnesota, the Teton Sioux of the Great Plains lived a good life. They were fine hunters, and buffalo were so plentiful that they rarely knew the pinch of want. They were great warriors, too, and their five main divisions — Ogalalas, Hunkpapas, Sans Arcs, Brulés, and Minneconjous — almost always had war parties out against their enemies, the Crows, Pawnees, Shoshones, and other tribes.

Superb horsemen, owning many fine ponies, they wandered wherever the whim moved them. A kind of wild chivalry prevailed among them. A deed of valor was more admired than mere damage inflicted on the foe, and often when a brave enemy was captured, he was adopted into the tribe.

When the California gold strike came, and the Overland Trail was cut deep into the prairie sod by thousands of wagons, the Indians at first drew back in astonishment from that surge of vehicles and white men. Then, since horses were considered objects of capture, they ran off some livestock. This led to shootings, and that to attacks on wagon trains.

Presently the army took a hand. On August 19, 1854, Lieutenant John L. Grattan, with thirty men, entered the Brulé Sioux village of Whirling Bear to seize an Indian accused of butchering an ox belonging to a white man. Whirling Bear objected that the ox was wandering loose and unowned. When the other Sioux showed defiance, Grattan ordered his men to fire. In the instant battle that followed, every soldier, including Grattan, lost his life, although one managed to reach Fort Laramie and tell what happened, before he died two or three days later.

The angry Sioux surrounded and threatened the fort itself, cut off a mail party, and killed two or three white men. In the skirmishing, Whirling Bear was slain. Another chief, Little Thunder, led the band 100 miles down the Platte River to a place called Ash Hollow.

There, September 3, they were attacked by General W. S. Harney, with 1200 men. Eighty-six Sioux were killed, including women and children. Harney lost only four dead and seven wounded. Plundered mail, clothing from Grattan's slain men, and the scalps of two white women were found in the camp. Thoroughly routed, the Indians scattered.

Strangely, the Sioux as a people did not follow this up with a general war. Perhaps they thought the Brulés had received punishment that they in some manner deserved. In any case, they moved north to the Powder River country of Wyoming, far from the wagon trail.

But the curse of gold pursued the red men. It was found in Montana in 1862, and thousands of miners rushed thither. Mining camps sprang up, and there was need for supplies. A trail, over which wagons could go to the gold fields from Fort Laramie, Wyoming, to Virginia City, Montana, was worked out by John M. Bozeman in 1865.

The difficulty with the Bozeman Trail was that it led through the heart of the Sioux country. Therefore the government offered treaties to the Sioux, to gain permission to use this trail. With that a great and spectacular figure rose to immediate prominence among the Indians.

His name was Red Cloud, and in 1865 he was forty-three years old. His father, an Ogalala of no distinction, died a drunkard; but the son did not follow his

Red Cloud

father's steps. Very early he made a name as a skillful hunter, a magnificent horseman, and a bold warrior. We have many photographs of him — a tall man with a deeply lined face, the strong nose and grim mouth showing leadership and determination, the narrowed eyes indicating cunning and foresight.

Red Cloud opposed permission for use of the trail, pointing out that the wagons would scare away the game and ruin the Sioux hunting grounds. At a great council, June 30, 1866, in Fort Laramie, he denounced Colonel Henry B. Carrington, who had been sent to build forts along the route — so sure was the government that it was going to get its treaty. Pointing to the silver eagles on the officer's shoulder straps, Red Cloud shouted that he was "the white eagle who has come to steal a road through the Indians' land." Then he ordered his followers to strike their tepees and left, saying he would fight if the white men tried to use the trail.

After a little hesitation the other Sioux bands followed him. By his defiant stand Red Cloud had become the greatest chief among them. Along Little Goose River (near present-day Sheridan, Wyoming) the Indian encampment extended for miles, and it was estimated that 15,000 persons, of whom 4000 were warriors, were there.

Yet, whether the Sioux liked it or not, the government had decided to establish forts along the trail. Carrington marched north, built and garrisoned Fort Reno, then moved on to erect a post called Fort Phil Kearny on Piney Creek (between Sheridan and Buffalo, Wyoming), while a detachment went still farther to build Fort C. F. Smith on the Bighorn River.

Construction on Fort Phil Kearny began July 15. Less than forty-eight hours later, at daybreak, July 17, the Sioux made their first attack. They stampeded a herd of the post's horses, and killed two and wounded three soldiers. Later that day they killed six men of a small wagon train. In the next twelve days five other wagon trains were attacked, fifteen men killed, and much livestock run off. Carrington wrote for reinforcements on July 24 — in a single week he had learned how implacable was his enemy.

The Sioux were described by General George A. Crook as "the finest natural cavalry that ever existed." Yet, since mobility was one of their greatest traits, they were not well fitted for conducting a lengthy siege. They had little organization, no discipline, and no knowledge of scientific warfare. In spite of this, because of Red Cloud's remorseless will, they besieged Fort Phil Kearny for two years.

Nothing like it was ever done by Indians, except Pontiac's siege of Detroit. About the fort prowled ceaselessly watchful war parties, and the soldiers found they had a foe who never slept. A herder who strayed or a sentry who exposed himself was laid low. Any detachment that went forth without strong numbers straightway had to fight for its life. Even during the long, bitter cold spells of Wyoming winter, the Indians kept about the post a circle of death.

In the first five and a half months, from July 15 to December 31, 1866, the Sioux killed 154 men at or near Fort Phil Kearny, wounded 21, and captured 700 head of livestock. In that time they made 51 separate hostile demonstrations.

Yet, in this constant peril, the men worked doggedly at building the fort. The country about was hilly but barren, and the nearest forests from which stockade posts could be cut were seven miles away. Carrington planned a huge enclosure, 1600 feet long by 600 wide, with forty-two buildings, all of logs. Wood parties constantly felled timber and hauled it to the fort, always with rifles close at hand and guards under arms. These parties sometimes numbered 150 men, but they never left the fort without dreading an attack by the Sioux.

A new officer, Captain William J. Fetterman, arrived in November with a company of cavalry. Rash and overconfident, Fetterman from the first thought Carrington too cautious, and demanded action. He got action — on December 6, when he foolishly pursued a decoy party of Sioux riders, was cut off, and was barely saved after Carrington arrived with more soldiers.

Though he lost seven men in that encounter, the fire-eating Fetterman was not convinced. Shortly afterward, he boasted, "Give me eighty men and I'll ride through the whole Sioux Nation!"

His opportunity came, December 21. That morning the lookout on Pilot Hill, south of the fort, frantically wigwagged that the wood train was being attacked. Fetterman asked to command the relief detachment, which consisted, besides himself, of 78 officers and men, and 2 armed civilians — exactly the number of his boast.

Out of the fort they rode with Carrington's final orders in their ears: "Relieve the wood train, drive back the Indians, *but on no account pursue the Indians beyond Lodge Trail Ridge.*"

Fetterman thought he knew better than his superior. Riding to Lodge Trail Ridge, northwest of the fort, he occupied it. The lookout on Pilot Hill wigwagged that the wood train no longer was being attacked. Fetterman should have returned at once. Instead, to the alarm of watchers at the fort, he and his men disappeared over the other side of the ridge.

He had fallen victim to a trap laid with uncanny skill. Below him he saw a handful of Indians so tantalizingly near he could not resist the impulse to pursue them. How was he to know that in ravines on either side of the path over which he was being led, hundreds of Sioux and Cheyenne warriors lay hidden. The ten Indians he saw were picked braves, chosen as a high honor for the dangerous work of acting as decoys. One of them was a young Ogalala named Crazy Horse, just beginning to build his reputation as the greatest of Sioux fighters.

Down the hill dashed Fetterman and his men, and up the lower ridge beyond (now called Massacre Hill). Whipping their horses back and forth in front of the

soldiers, the ten Indians retreated until they reached the trap in the draw beyond, and saw their pursuers were in its jaws.

Then a flight of arrows glinted like grasshoppers in the sunlight, and with a wild yelping of war whoops, the Indians from the two ravines swept out and swirled about the soldiers. Some troopers were killed in the first charge. Others tried to retreat up the ridge. But in a final great rush of flashing lances, tomahawks, and clubs, with rifles adding to the uproar, they were slain to a man. Fetterman's boast had proved empty, and bitterly tragic.

At the fort, cut off from view by Lodge Trail Ridge, listeners heard the great noise of guns and yelling, which continued for some time, then ceased. What had happened? Were the Indians beaten off, or the soldiers defeated? Nobody dreamed of the extent of the disaster until a relief party under Captain T. Ten Eyck reached the scene. Some Indians still were galloping about, but they soon withdrew. All that remained was the ghastly evidence of the calamity — 81 dead bodies, including Fetterman's. The Indians later said they lost 12 killed and 60 wounded.

The temperature was falling as the bodies were carried back to the fort. That night a terrific blizzard broke. But for that blizzard the Sioux might have overwhelmed the fort itself, for the defenders were gravely reduced in numbers and ammunition was low. As it was, that night Carrington ordered every woman and child placed in the powder magazine, with an officer sworn not to allow a single one to fall alive into the Indians' hands. If the fort was captured, he was to blow up the magazine with all in it.

The Indians, however, did not attack. So cold was it — the thermometer went down to thirty degrees below zero — that they stayed close to their warm tepees. Carrington asked for a volunteer to carry a message for help. John Phillips, a scout, commonly called "Portugee," stepped forward.

Starting at dark, he led his horse for miles to get beyond the Indian cordon. Then he mounted, and his epic ride through the swirling blizzard is one of the legends of the West. Before he reached Fort Laramie, 236 miles away, he rode his horse to death. He himself was almost dead as he staggered into the officers' club the night of December 24 and broke up a Christmas Eve dance with his dread news.

The nation was shocked. Reinforcements and ammunition were hurried to Phil Kearny. Though he was not to blame for the disaster, Carrington was replaced in command by Lieutenant Colonel H. H. Wessells.

Among the new weapons brought to the fort by the relief column was a shipment of the latest-type fire-arms — Springfield-Allen rapid-fire rifles. They played a spectacular role in the next meeting with Red Cloud.

All next spring and summer the Sioux hectored the post, but on August 2, 1867, they attempted another blow akin to the Fetterman victory. This time they chose to wipe out the wood train and its escort.

Captain James Powell, commanding the escort, knew great danger threatened that morning, when a daring band of braves stampeded the wood train horse herd. The horse guards and some of the wood choppers escaped to the fort, but four men were killed and scalped in the woods.

Powell ordered fourteen wagon bodies dismounted from the wood haulers' vehicles, and dragged into an oval corral, in the middle of an open space about 1000 yards across. The tops of the wagon beds were covered with blankets so the movements of those within could not be seen. Here he gathered all who were not dead, or escaped to the fort — thirty-two men. By rare good fortune, they were all armed with the new rifles. Coolly he told off the best shots and ordered the others to load for them.

Out on the plain rode a great cloud of warriors, vivid in paint, feathered headdresses, and flashing weapons, yelling their war cries. The wagon-box cor-

ral squatted in the open, silent, apparently empty, yet menacing.

How many men were within the Sioux did not know, but they thought they could ride it down in a single rush. Red Cloud himself waved a blanket over his head. At the signal, 1200 savage horsemen charged in a thundering, yelling, galloping mass.

From the wagon boxes a sudden volley crashed, emptying many Indian saddles. On charged the rest. But to their amazement, instead of the usual pause to reload before a second volley, a continuous stream of lead poured from the corral. Down went some of their best warriors. The charge split and roared by on either side of the wagon boxes.

Baffled, the Sioux drew off. That steady fire — they had never faced rapid-shooting rifles before — made them think more men were in that corral than they had supposed. Only a comparative few of the Indians had guns, and though the wagon beds were furred with arrows, the defenders had lost only three killed in the charge.

For a time the Sioux who had firearms tried to subdue the corral by gunfire, creeping up through the grass and bushes. But they did little damage, most of their bullets going too high. So infrequently did the white men reply that the Indians believed they had killed most of them.

After a time they charged again, this time on foot — a wedge of naked, painted bodies, fluttering war bonnets, and waving weapons. But again from the wagon boxes came the blast of flame and lead. The center of the wedge was eaten out by the ceaseless bullets, and the Indians again fell back.

It took the heart out of the savages. They tried one more charge, but it fell short. Late in the afternoon a column of soldiers under Major John E. Smith arrived from the fort with a howitzer. At the boom of the big gun, and the sight of the blue uniforms, the Sioux retired, carrying their dead and wounded. The rescuers could hardly believe their eyes when Powell and his men crawled out of the wagon boxes.

It was a spectacular and bloody victory over the savages. Including the four woodchoppers killed in the woods, the white loss was seven dead and three wounded. Captain Powell estimated 180 Indians killed or wounded — very likely a close guess, since he had seen many battlefields during the Civil War and could judge losses by experience.

The Wagon Box Fight was a blow to Red Cloud, but he hung on grimly. And the following spring his determination was rewarded. A treaty commission met with the Sioux, April 29, 1868. Red Cloud was the central figure, and his terms were final: government forts must be abandoned, and the Bozeman Trail closed.

On the agreement that the Sioux would not interfere with the building of the transcontinental railroad then being laid — far south of their hunting grounds — the government ceded "in perpetuity" the Black Hills and the entire Powder River country to the Sioux.

Red Cloud had won the war — one of the few wars ever won by the red men against whites.

That August, in full view of hundreds of Sioux, the soldiers at Fort Phil Kearny hauled down the colors and marched out of the post they had built and defended at such cost. As soon as they were gone, the Sioux entered, and a black pillar of smoke, as they set

the place ablaze, marked Red Cloud's great triumph.

Red Cloud signed the peace treaty and forever kept it. He died in 1909, when he was eighty-five years old. Though he was then feeble and nearly blind, he was described by one who knew him well as "a most courtly chief and a natural-born gentleman, with a bow as graceful as that of a Chesterfield."

He won his war, but he foresaw that there would be other wars, not so fortunate for his people. Struggle as they might, the Indians could never hold back the inevitable advance of the white man. There was too much to gain in the West — farms and ranches, mines

and timber, which must be turned to valuable production.

Always he counseled the Indians against fighting. It did no good — they fought, bravely but in the end fruitlessly. Indeed they hardly ceased fighting, and within less than ten years they were to meet their enemy in the most famous Indian battle of all time, on a stream hardly known until then, called the Little Bighorn.

But that was in the future, and we must now go back a little in time, for the beginnings of another part of our history, closely connected with the Sioux, but concerning the fortunes of another tribe.

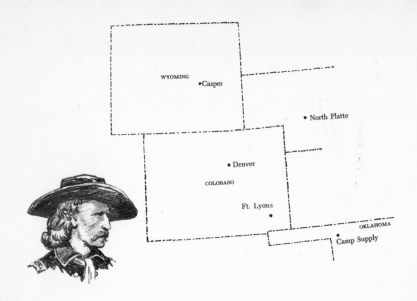

The Brave and Unlucky Cheyennes | 5

IT WAS COLD in barren eastern Colorado, November 28, 1864. Patches of snow showed here and there in the gullies among the dry buffalo grass and clumps of sagebrush. But all day long a trailing column of blue — cavalry — had moved steadily across the landscape.

Toward nightfall there was a halt. A group of officers spurred forward to where a half-breed Indian sat on his horse, his bridle reins tied to a soldier's saddle. He was Jack Smith, son of a white trapper by a Cheyenne woman, and he had been kidnaped to guide this foray.

The commanding officer rasped out a question, and the soldier saluted, for it was Colonel J. M. Chivington, of the 2nd Colorado Cavalry.

"The breed won't go any farther, sir," he said.

"Wolf, he howl," said the Indian. "Injun dog, he hear wolf, he howl too. Injun, he hear dog an' listen; hear something an' run off."

He glanced hopefully at Chivington, but the colonel's face was dark with rage. "Jack," he said, "if you fool with me, and don't lead me to that camp —" He tapped his revolver holster. The unhappy guide, who had hoped to save his people, sighed and led on.

It should be said here that the Indian-fighting army of the West often was the best friend the Indians had. Officers like Generals Crook, Howard, and Miles, and many of their subordinates, both officers and men, understood the red men better than did most civilians. They tried to avoid war and bloodshed whenever possible, and when they did fight, it was because of some necessity, either due to the misdeeds of civilians, or to some hotheaded war-hungry Indian leader. They did their duty as splendid fighters, but first and last they helped the savage people as much as they could.

Chivington was not of this class, however. He was a former preacher, who had made a name as a bull-headed fighter against the Confederates in New Mexico. A religious fanatic, he agreed with the saying, "The only good Indian is a dead Indian." Before he went "Indian hunting" on this occasion, he showed his ferocity, when in a public speech he said, "Kill and scalp all [Indians] big and little; nits make lice."

Who were Chivington and his 900 "ninety-day men" hunting that cold November day? There had been raids on the stage lines, and he was hunting Indians — *any* Indians. But the village to which Jack Smith was ordered to lead them was Cheyenne, and it happened that its people were not on the warpath but at peace with the white men.

Of the horseback Indians of the West, none were finer than the Cheyennes. Their name was a white spelling of the Sioux word *Shai-ena* — "People of Alien Speech" — and for generations they had been friends and allies of the Sioux. Well-dressed, handsome, brave, they were famed for their horsemanship, their pretty women, and the valor of their warriors.

They were among the first to oppose the pushing out of white people across the plains, and so persistently did they harry wagon trains that in 1857 Colonel E. V. Sumner set out to subdue them. What followed was one of the greatest fiascos in Indian-fighting history.

Sumner, with nine companies of cavalry, found 300 Cheyenne warriors drawn up in the Smoky Hill River valley of Kansas. Bugles sang, and the cavalry, drawing their flashing sabers, made a grand charge, horses careering, men cheering — a splendid sight to see.

The only trouble was that the enemy was not there to enjoy the sight.

With one astonished glance, the Cheyennes left. "Their horses were fresh, and very fleet," ruefully reported Sumner, "and it was impossible to overtake very many of them." That was the last time Indian-fighting cavalry carried sabers. Carbines and revolvers did far better execution.

Skirmishes and attacks on wagon trains and ranches continued. When the Civil War began in 1861, the attention of the nation turned from the frontier, and it grew so hard to get provisions from the East to Denver that the people in the Colorado mining towns suffered. Naturally, their resentment turned against the Indians whose raids made it so difficult to get food and goods across the plains.

It must be admitted that the Cheyennes took part in those raids. But so did the fierce Kiowas, Comanches, Arapahoes, and even a few bands of Sioux (this was before Red Cloud's War). As for the Cheyennes, they had ceased their forays, and the hostilities that so enraged the Colorado people that fall were not their doing.

The previous August, of 1864, the famous trader William Bent, who had a Cheyenne wife and several half-Cheyenne children, persuaded the tribe to make peace. To prove their friendly intentions, the villages of Black Kettle and White Antelope surrendered half their firearms at Fort Lyon, Colorado, keeping only enough for hunting. They were told to camp on Big Sandy Creek, thirty miles north of the fort, where they were assured they would be safe. An American flag was given them to display, to show they were peaceful.

It was on this village that Chivington was marching.

He continued his march all that night. At daybreak, November 29, 1864, a squaw in the Cheyenne camp on the Big Sandy heard a distant rumble of hoofs. She cried out that buffalo were coming. Not until the Indians rushed out of their tepees and saw the blue uniforms did they know that troops were in the vicinity.

At first the Cheyennes could not believe that the white men meant war. Black Kettle ran up the American flag over his tepee, with a white flag above it. The warriors, surprised and unprepared, huddled together.

A sputter of gunshots — and Chivington's cavalry charged!

What followed was a dreadful and disgraceful massacre. Women and children were slain without mercy. Old White Antelope stood with his arms folded, singing his death song, until he was shot down. Black Kettle and some of his warriors fought a rear-guard battle to help their people escape. But Cheyennes were killed by scores. In that bloody day about 160 of them died, of whom only 60 could be called warriors.

As a crowning infamy, the poor unwilling guide, Jack Smith, was murdered by the soldiers. Then, having looted the village, Chivington and his men returned in great triumph to Denver, where they were cheered when they displayed, between acts at a theatrical performance, about 100 scalps they had taken.

To its credit, the government repudiated the act. In 1868 a military commission appointed by Congress to investigate it, and containing three famous generals, William Tecumseh Sherman, Alfred H. Terry, and C. C. Augur, besides civilians of the highest standing, made this sweeping condemnation of Chivington and his massacre:

It scarcely has its parallel in records of Indian barbarity. Fleeing women, holding up their hands and praying for mercy were shot down; infants were killed and scalped in derision; men were tortured and mutilated . . . No one will be astonished that a war ensued which cost the government $30,000,000 and carried conflagration and death to the border settlements. During the spring and summer of 1865 no less than 8,000 troops were withdrawn from the effective forces engaged against the Rebellion to meet this Indian war.

The government paid the Cheyennes an indemnity — as if that could repay them for the lives of their people. Chivington became an object of public scorn. He died obscure and poor.

Never did the Cheyennes forget the slaughter that has come down in history as the Sand Creek Massacre. They carried the war pipe north to the Sioux. One Sioux chief who smoked the war pipe was Sitting Bull. From that day he was the white man's bitter foe. It can be said that Custer's terrible defeat at the Little Bighorn had its roots in Sand Creek.

Next summer, 1865, the Cheyenne war parties scourged the frontier. As usual, the innocent often paid for the crimes of the guilty. Scores of white men and women, who had nothing to do with Chivington or Sand Creek, were killed by the furious Indians. Stage stations were destroyed all up and down the line, and for a time the stage route was completely closed. Wagon trains were captured and looted, and Julesburg, Colorado, was burned to the ground.

On one occasion an army paymaster's wagon, carrying thousands of dollars in greenbacks to pay the Colorado troops, was captured near Julesburg. Not knowing the value of the "green paper," the Indians had a

gleeful time scattering it all over the valley and twisting it into their ponies' manes and tails for ornaments.
Next day when the paymaster with a military detail
from Fort Rankin tried to recover the money, it was
found strewn for a mile or more. Only about half of it
was ever recovered.

In the middle of that summer the Cheyennes moved
north, and appeared near a fort guarding a bridge
across the Platte River (where Casper, Wyoming, now
stands). On July 26, 1865, a supply train with a small
escort was heading for the fort, and Lieutenant Caspar
Collins was sent with a detachment to bring it in.
Down on him swooped the Indians, killed Collins and
eight of his twenty-five men, and drove the rest, some
of them badly wounded, back to the fort.

Meantime, Sergeant Amos J. Custard, commanding
the wagon train, heard the firing and sent five
men forward to see what it was. Two of these were
killed; the other three hid in the brush of the Platte
River bottom, and finally managed to reach the fort
alive.

Not so fortunate were the sergeant and his nineteen
remaining men. As the Cheyennes, with some Sioux,
rode toward them, Custard corralled his wagons, and
opened fire. A number of warriors were knocked out
of their saddles, and the rest drew back out of range.

Now a gigantic warrior with a handsome war bonnet appeared and rode slowly all the way around the wagon corral, studying it. He was Roman Nose, the most noted Cheyenne fighter. His proper name was Sauts (the Bat), but his nose was hooked like the beak of some fierce bird of prey, and the white men called him Roman Nose. Six feet three inches tall, and weighing a muscular 230 pounds, he was equaled in strength or courage by few Indians. Habitually he took great risks in battle, for he believed that the sacred war bonnet he wore protected him from enemy bullets.

After his leisurely survey, Roman Nose had his braves dismount, creep up close, and pour a terribly destructive fire into the wagons. About three o'clock in the afternoon the Indians stopped shooting. All alone, Roman Nose rode around the wagon corral, very close, to draw fire. Not a shot answered his challenge.

Then Roman Nose dared, all alone, to enter the corral. Every soldier was dead or badly wounded. The Cheyennes rushed in and killed all who were living. The two fights near Platte Bridge cost the troops twenty-nine lives. The supply train furnished the Cheyennes badly needed munitions.

All through 1866 the Cheyennes were in the north, helping Red Cloud's Sioux against Fort Phil Kearny. They took a leading part in the destruction of Fetterman's command. But in 1867 they were back on the southern plains, raiding. General W. S. Hancock took the field with 1100 men, to show the Indians that "the government is ready and able to punish them if they are hostile."

The Cheyennes laughed at his clumsy expedition, played will-o'-the-wisp with it, and after four months of fruitless marching and countermarching, Hancock returned with his exhausted troops to Fort Harker, Kansas.

One of his officers was a dashing young cavalryman, fresh from the East, and destined to leave a tragic name in history — Lieutenant Colonel George Armstrong Custer. Custer pursued the Indians with energy, but without effect — indeed he lost a detachment

of eleven men under Lieutenant Kidder, all of whom were cut off and killed.

With interest the Cheyennes had watched the building of the Union Pacific Railroad across their prairies. That summer they tried an experiment. Somewhere east of North Platte, Nebraska, they pulled the spikes out of a rail and bent it out of line. Then they hid to see what happened.

Late at night a glaring light appeared from the east — the headlight of the engine of a freight train. As it rushed along, the locomotive struck the bent rail, jumped the track, and turned over. Every man in the crew was killed, either in the wreck, or by the Indians. The train was looted.

If 1867 was bad, however, 1868 was worse. Twenty-five raids took place that summer on settlements in Kansas, Colorado, and Texas, with 117 persons killed and 7 women carried into captivity. Not an Indian was slain in these affairs.

So desperate became the situation that General Phil Sheridan took the field in person. He soon saw how impossible it was for ordinary soldiers to try to follow the Indians. But there were plenty of experienced frontiersmen available, and when Major George A. Forsyth suggested that he might enlist a battalion of scouts, to play their own game with the Indians, Sheridan gave him authority to do so.

Forsyth soon enrolled fifty hard-bitten Indian fighters, and with this cocksure handful he rode out of Fort Wallace, Kansas, September 10, 1868. They were armed with the latest seven-shooter Spencer carbines, and they believed they could whip any number of Indians they might meet.

Two days out of Fort Wallace, they struck a big Indian trail, and hotly followed it until they reached the Arikaree River, just west of the Kansas line in Colorado, September 16. The river had a wide sandy bottom, with a small stream of water meandering down it, and in its bed was an island covered with plum brush. They did not know that they were on the trail of Roman Nose's Cheyennes — much less that the Indians knew all about them, and were preparing for them — or they might not have slept so well when they camped there that night.

Just at the first streak of dawn next morning, September 17, a shot echoed out, and with it a yell: *"Indians!"* At the same moment the entire horizon seemed to fill with tossing war bonnets on which the first rays of the sun gleamed brilliantly.

"Down to that island!" shouted Forsyth.

Helter-skelter, pell-mell, his men rode for it, threw themselves from their horses, and began frantically to burrow small rifle pits in the sand under the plum bushes. The menacing array of Indians spread across the valley from side to side. Old plainsmen distinguished not only Cheyennes, but Arapahoes and Brulé Sioux in that warlike mass of horsemen.

Suddenly, as if at a signal, the Indians drummed their heels against their horses' sides, and charged — a screaming wave of death.

"Hold your fire until they're within fifty yards!" Forsyth ordered. On the island his scouts obeyed, glancing down their gun barrels, but not pressing a trigger, as the fearsome horde bore down upon them.

As the imaginary line was crossed, Forsyth spoke a single word: *"Now!"*

Instantly the island blazed with flame and smoke,

and the seven-shooters never ceased pouring lead into the Indian ranks. Down went braves and horses, some turning crashing somersaults as they fell at full career. The Indian charge — as in the Wagon Box Fight — broke in the middle and thundered off down the river-bed on either side of the rifle pits.

The first onset was broken. But the Indians were not through. Chiefs galloped about, giving orders. Some braves slipped forward on foot to keep up a fire on the scouts from some willow bushes south of the island. But these were presently driven off.

Forsyth, wounded in three places, counted his loss. Of 51 officers and men, 23 were dead or wounded, including Lieutenant Frederick Beecher, second in command, who was dying.

Roman Nose did not take part in the morning fight. One of the charms connected with his sacred war bonnet was that he must not eat food taken from the pot with an iron utensil. The night before the battle, at a feast, he ate meat served by a squaw with an iron fork. He did not notice this until too late, and since he had no time for purification ceremonies before the fight began, he believed that if he faced the enemy now he would die. This is the story of the Indians themselves, although Forsyth believed Roman Nose was killed in the first charge and said so in an article he later wrote.

Such a power was the giant chief that the other Cheyennes begged him to lead them. In the afternoon he at last agreed, put on his war bonnet, mounted, and with a wave of his great arm, summoned his warriors.

This time, if Roman Nose lived, the charge would be driven home. Down on the desperate handful on the island thundered the galloping horde. Nothing, it seemed, could halt it.

Suddenly, just before the island was reached, a bullet brought the mighty leader crashing out of his saddle. The whole Indian array jolted to a stop, then rode away, taking along the body of the dying chief.

In the two charges they had lost about 100 warriors, according to Forsyth's estimate. Yet for days they besieged the island. Finally, at great peril, two pairs of scouts slipped through the hostile lines at night to get help. Forsyth's survivors, nearly dead of starvation, were saved by the arrival of the 10th Cavalry, September 26.

That fall Sheridan decided to attack the Indians in their winter camps. He gave his reasons as follows:

Not less than 800 persons had been murdered, the Indians escaping from the troops by traveling at night when their trail could not be followed, thus gaining enough time and distance to render pursuit, in most cases, fruitless . . . In the winter the savages would hide away in their villages, in remote and isolated places, to live upon their plunder, glory in the scalps taken, and in the horrible debasement of unfortunate women they held as prisoners . . . To disabuse their minds of the idea that they were secure from punishment . . . a winter campaign was projected against the large bands hiding away in the Indian Territory.

Lieutenant Colonel Custer, who was given the job, was probably the most picturesque figure in our military history. He loved theatrical display, wore his yellow hair in long curls, practically designed his own uniforms, sought publicity, and wrote magazine articles to popularize himself as an Indian fighter. He had distinguished himself in the Civil War, becoming a brevet major general of volunteers when only twenty-six years old.

With the 7th Cavalry, Custer marched south from Camp Supply (present Supply, Oklahoma), November 22, 1868, in a bitter cold snap, with a foot of snow on the ground. On November 26 he found the trail of a war party, which he followed until that night his scouts discovered in the valley of the Washita River the dying embers of a fire kindled by Indian herd boys. They were close to an Indian village.

It chanced to be the village of Black Kettle — the same that was attacked by Chivington at Sand Creek. Other Indian villages lay up and down the river — Cheyennes, Kiowas, Arapahoes, Comanches, and Lipan Apaches. Had he known that, Custer might not have attacked, but it was Black Kettle's misfortune that the troops found his village at night.

In the darkness Custer divided his men into four detachments and quietly surrounded the camp. At dawn, November 27, a bugle sounded the charge, and the cavalry rushed down upon the doomed village.

It was another massacre. Black Kettle and his wife were killed in front of their lodge. Others died in the camp, while some ran naked onto the ice-covered river to escape. By ten o'clock the fighting seemed over. There were 100 dead Indians, including many women and children, and 53 squaws and children were captives.

But then, to his surprise, Custer saw hundreds of warriors riding up the valley. They were from the lower villages, coming to help Black Kettle — too late. Custer was forced to beat a retreat, after killing 700 captured ponies. He had lost 2 officers and 19 men dead, and 3 officers and 11 men wounded.

The bloody attack on the Washita was a terrible blow to the Cheyennes. But already a new war was brewing to the north, and in that war the Cheyennes would avenge their stricken village against the very men who had struck the blow — Custer and his 7th Cavalry.

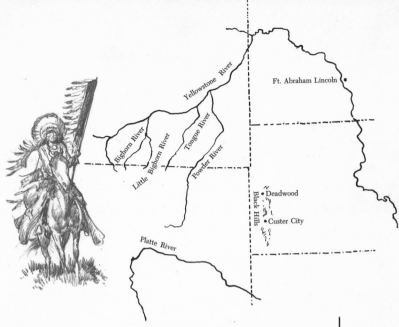

The Most Famous Indian Battle | 6

In the summer of 1875 the Sioux were furious. About
their council fires famous warriors talked war, and in
the sun dances more than the usual number of young
men went through the ordeal of self-torture that initi-
ated them into full rank as braves.

The reason for this anger, this gathering of weapons,
this war talk was that the solemn promises of the government, made in a treaty, had been violated. It was
added fuel to the Indians' rage that the violation had
been the act of a man they had especial reason to hate
— that same Custer who butchered the Cheyennes on
the banks of the icebound Washita River.

Since Red Cloud's War, there had been peace of a
sort between the Sioux and the white man, although on

the southern plains the Comanches, Kiowas, and Cheyennes fought some sharp battles before they were forced on their reservations in the Indian Territory, in 1874.

In that same year — 1874 — Custer, with his 7th Cavalry, had "explored" the Black Hills of Dakota and had come out trumpeting that gold was there. The Black Hills were sacred to the Sioux, and the government had guaranteed to keep white people out. But it could not control its citizens. A gold stampede began, the Black Hills swarmed with prospectors and miners, and Deadwood, Custer City, and other mining towns sprang up like mushrooms.

How could the Sioux be blamed for anger? By thousands they left their Agencies. Out in the Powder River country their bands camped in the circles of old time, and held ceaseless powwows, always concerning war.

By the summer of 1875 two Sioux chiefs had come to the forefront among their people. Their names were Sitting Bull and Crazy Horse, and it is worth the time to consider them here.

In all respects Sitting Bull, of the Hunkpapas, was a remarkable Indian. Born in 1834, he was a famous warrior while still in his twenties, but it was not as a fighter that he was chiefly important to his people. He was a leader and organizer, who better than any could keep them together. John F. Finerty, who saw him in Canada in 1879, thus described him:

His hair, parted in the ordinary Sioux fashion, was without a plume. His broad face, with prominent hooked nose and wide jaws, was destitute of paint. His fierce, half-bloodshot eyes gleamed from under brows which displayed large perceptive organs, and, as he . . . regarded me with a look which seemed blended of curiosity and insolence, I did not need to be told that he was Sitting Bull . . . I noticed that he was an inch or two over medium height, broadly built, rather bow-legged . . . and he limped slightly as from an old wound.

If Sitting Bull was the greatest organizer of the Sioux, Crazy Horse was one of their all-time greatest warriors. A tragic and heroic figure, he combined in himself most of the virtues of his people. Born in 1844, he was only twenty-one when the siege of Fort Phil Kearny began, but he was one of the principal leaders in the Fetterman and Wagon Box Fights. Though an Ogalala, he so won the admiration of the Cheyennes that at times he had more of that tribe than his own people in his camp. Here is how he appeared to Captain John G. Bourke, after he surrendered in 1877:

I saw before me a man who looked quite young . . .
five feet, eight inches high, lithe and sinewy, with a scar
on his face. The expression on his face was one of quiet
dignity, but . . . dogged, tenacious, and melancholy . . .
All Indians gave him a high reputation for courage and
generosity. In advancing upon an enemy, none of his
warriors were allowed to pass him . . . He had made
hundreds of friends by his charity to the poor, as it was
a point of honor with him never to keep anything for
himself, except weapons of war. I never heard an Indian
mention his name, save in terms of respect.

Such were Sitting Bull and Crazy Horse, the leaders
of their people, and the real driving forces in the
Sioux War of 1876–1877.

In November, 1875, the government became so
alarmed over the unrest of the Sioux that General
Alfred H. Terry sent word to Sitting Bull, telling him
to bring his people in to the reservation by January 1,
or he would "come looking for him."

Back came a haughty reply from the chief: "You
won't need to bring guides. You can find me easily.
I won't run away."

That winter was very cold, the worst in years, and
the Indians could hardly have moved in any event.
Nevertheless, troops were put in motion. March 17,
1876, Colonel Joseph J. Reynolds, with ten troops of

Crazy Horse

Sitting Bull

cavalry, struck a village near the mouth of the Little Powder River in Montana.

It was Crazy Horse's village. To the Indians, Reynolds' charge was a complete surprise. Out of their tepees burst the Sioux, many of them naked — the way Indians usually slept. The day was intensely cold, and at first the troops drove the red men and their families from the camp, burning their lodges and capturing their horse herd.

But they were dealing with Crazy Horse. The chief rallied his warriors and brought them back fighting. In a sharp, fierce battle, he forced Reynolds to retreat so rapidly that he abandoned his dead, while the Indians recaptured their horses. The affair resulted in a series of courts-martial, and several officers resigned their commissions.

March passed, and so did April. The snows cleared and the wild roses were budding. The army prepared a great pincer movement to crush the Sioux.

From Fort A. Lincoln (near Bismarck, North Dakota), General Terry marched west for the Yellowstone River, with a heavy force of cavalry, infantry, and three Gatling guns. At the same time General Crook headed north from Fort Fetterman on the Platte River in Wyoming. If they could catch the Indians in the jaws of that trap, the Sioux must be smashed.

Crook, an experienced Indian fighter who had gained fame battling the Apaches in Arizona, followed the trail Reynolds had taken, with 1200 men. Very soon he learned that Crazy Horse knew all about his march, for a warning came from that chief, telling the general not to cross the Tongue River, Montana, or he would be attacked. Just to prove he meant what he said, Crazy Horse's warriors fired on the soldiers, wounding two of them, when Crook reached the Tongue and camped there June 9.

That was not the battlefield Crazy Horse had chosen, however. Crook camped four days and was joined by nearly 300 Crow and Shoshone scouts, raising his force to 1500 fighting men. Then he crossed the Tongue and reached the Rosebud River, June 16, where he camped.

Next morning, June 17, with the Indian scouts ahead, the march was resumed down the river. By midmorning Crook reached a place where the valley widened into a sort of amphitheater, surrounded on all sides by bluffs. Suddenly shots were heard ahead. A moment later the Indian scouts came careering down over the bluffs, riding for life, and yelling, "Sioux! Sioux! Heap Sioux!"

A little later the same bluffs were crowned by hundreds of Indians in full war regalia. Rifles began crackling in the clear air. So many warriors were in sight that Crook knew he was dealing with Crazy Horse's main force.

While officers rallied the fleeing scouts, the troops wheeled into battle line and fired a heavy volley. Presently, Captain Anson Mills, on the right, and Captain W. B. Royall, on the left, led dashing cavalry charges to drive the Sioux from the bluffs. The Indians fell back, but beyond, on higher ground, they gathered so thickly and fiercely that the cavalry halted and sent back for reinforcements. Every man in Crook's force was now engaged, and more braves were arriving to join the Sioux.

All at once Crazy Horse took the offensive. A headlong charge of his warriors struck Crook's left.

Yelping like wolves, the Sioux rode right into Royall's trooper line, horses and soldiers falling. Then the whole mass, Indians and white men, in a welter of dust and smoke, went rolling down the bluff together, fighting hand-to-hand.

At this critical moment a countercharge by Captain Guy V. Henry and his company saved the situation. But Henry was shot and wounded, and for a time a bloody melee was fought over his body, where he fell from his horse. The bravery of Washakie, chief of the Shoshone scouts, who rallied his braves to defend the captain, saved Henry's life. He lived to serve with distinction in the army for many more years.

By now the soldiers and their Indian allies had

retreated from the bluffs, carrying their wounded. To the right of the battle line, the Rosebud plunged into a deep and gloomy gorge called Dead Canyon. Thinking the Indian village might be at the other end of the gorge, Crook sent Mills down into it with three troops of cavalry.

Hardly had they entered the canyon, however, than the general recalled them. It was well he did so, for Crazy Horse had prepared an ambush in it from which none of Mills's command might have escaped alive.

Crook had been badly mauled. He had many wounded, besides the dead, and it was clear he could not handle the Sioux before him. Next day he retreated toward his base of supplies.

Crazy Horse had won a victory, the more remarkable since less than half his warriors were armed with guns. Crook was disposed of, for the present.

But there remained the other jaw of the pincer — Terry's force.

After the Battle of the Rosebud, Crazy Horse and Sitting Bull moved their people over the divide into the valley of the Little Bighorn River, where their great camp was pitched by the stream among the trees, extending for three miles. All the chief bands of Teton Sioux were there — Ogalalas, Hunkpapas, Sans Arcs, Minneconjous, and Brulés. Cheyennes and

Arapahoes were in the camp also, and there were refugees from Little Crow's Minnesota Santees.

By June 22 Terry had reached the mouth of the Rosebud on the Yellowstone River. His plan was to catch the hostiles between his column and that of Crook, but he did not know that Crook already had been defeated.

Terry believed the Sioux were concentrated somewhere between the Rosebud and the Bighorn River, possibly on the Little Bighorn. To find the Indians, if possible, he detached Lieutenant Colonel Custer and the 7th Cavalry, but with instructions that if the enemy was in too great force Custer was to wait for reinforcements from the main column, commanded by Terry himself, and under him, Colonel John Gibbon, and consisting of twelve companies of infantry, four troops of cavalry, and three Gatling guns, besides the pack and wagon trains of supplies.

Unfortunately, Custer was under the displeasure of President Grant because of some political activities. He was eager to do something brilliant to win back his lost favor. So when he found an Indian trail crossing over from the Rosebud to the Little Bighorn, he followed it without hesitation, reaching the valley of the latter at dawn, June 25.

Though he knew the Indians must be aware of his presence — one had been killed on his back trail, while another escaped to bear the news — Custer was exultantly sure of victory, when in the early sunlight he saw the smoke of an immense Indian village in the valley ahead.

"Custer's luck!" he exclaimed.

Then he broke his command into four detachments, to strike the village in different places. He had used such tactics successfully on the Washita, but at that fight he made his dispositions by night and attacked by surprise. Here he was dealing with an alert enemy in full daylight. Dividing his forces was his own death warrant, and the death warrants of many of his fine men.

Major F. W. Benteen with three troops was sent far to the left to encircle the southern end of the valley. Major Marcus A. Reno with three troops and most of the Arikara scouts rode straight down, followed by Captain Thomas MacDougall with one troop and the pack train. Custer himself, with the remaining five troops, went to the right, to take the village on the northern, or downstream, side.

More has been written, perhaps, about the Battle of the Little Bighorn — the most famous Indian battle of American history — than about any other single conflict in the United States, except the Battle of Gettysburg in the Civil War. Yet even today just what took place is not really known.

We do know that Reno crossed the river and found himself two miles above the village instead of near its center as he had expected. Turning to his right he trotted down the valley with his command.

Rifles began to flash ahead, and all at once the whole valley seemed filled by a yelling mass of savages. Reno halted, his men fired a volley, and then the charging Sioux forced them back into a thick grove of trees beside the river. The men dismounted and fought on foot. Meantime the Arikaras fled from the battlefield, except for a handful with the troops.

For a few minutes there was furious fighting among the trees. But the Sioux were gathering for another charge, rifle fire rose deafeningly, men were falling, and Reno ordered a retreat.

Some of his men did not hear. The others mounted and raced for safety, in a rout, while Indians, riding hard beside them, killed many. By the time they forded the river and reached the top of the bluffs on the other side, Reno had lost 3 officers and 29 enlisted men and scouts dead, 7 seriously wounded, and 15 missing—54 out of 112, almost half his command. (Later most of the missing men, who were left behind in the retreat, managed to join Reno on the bluffs.)

About this time Benteen arrived from the south, and soon afterward MacDougall and the pack train came in. Benteen had seen no Indians, but an hour before Trumpeter John Martini (the last to see Custer alive) had brought an urgent message from Custer. It read:

Benteen. Come on. Big village. Be quick. Bring packs. P.S. Bring packs.

Evidently Custer was in contact with the Indians and needed ammunition. But where was Custer?

For a time the Sioux, who crossed the river and were all about Reno, kept up a heavy fire on the soldiers, who were digging rifle pits. Then a strange thing happened. About three o'clock in the afternoon, as if at a signal, most of the savages suddenly galloped away toward the northwest.

Within a few minutes a tremendous roar of firing was heard in that direction. Custer was engaged at last!

Ominously, the uproar of battle increased in volume, and hung on the air, varying little in position. Officers and men on Reno's bluffs looked anxiously in that direction. Instead of a sudden, sharp attack, Custer must have a real battle on his hands. In fact — they could no longer conceal it from themselves — he must be fighting for his very life!

What happened to Custer has been pieced together, partly by evidence of the battlefield, partly on very unreliable and conflicting Indian testimony. Evidently he led his men to the crest of the ridge overlooking the main part of the village and then rode down to, or almost to, the river. He was there met by a few Indians, who opened fire.

At that Custer halted his men, to make sure what kind of opposition he faced, perhaps thinking a larger body of warriors faced him. Before he got into motion again, the Sioux who had been fighting Reno came streaming back — that was what had caused them to gallop away from Reno's bluffs.

A dense mass of warriors, with Crazy Horse at their head, beat the waters of the Little Bighorn into a foam as they charged across. Another body of braves, led by Gall, dashed up a dry coulee to one side.

Custer and his men began to fall back, fighting, toward the brow of the hill, which seemed a good place for defense. But before they reached the knob (where the monument on the battlefield now stands), a wave of warriors came over it and struck them. There, just below the crest, the bodies of Custer and many of his officers and men were later found.

One can only imagine the scene: the soldiers in blue, lying or standing along the ridge and down the slope, firing, some steadily, some wildly and hope-

lessly; the Indians, painted, stripped to their breech-clouts, in war bonnets or horned headgear, swirling about the doomed men on their horses, or charging into their ranks to knock them down, while more and still more came galloping up on lathered ponies from below; beyond this the river, showing here and there down in the valley among its trees, with the white cones of tepees visible in the glades; and over everything a pall of powder smoke and dust, and a din indescribably loud and hideous, of crashing guns, thundering hoofs, and whoops and yells and screams.

It was over in an hour. The Indian women came up from below to help the braves as they went over the field shooting or clubbing to death any white men yet living. Some they scalped, and they took clothing or anything else they valued from the bodies. Some of the dead they mutilated. The body of Custer, for some reason, they did not scalp or mutilate.

Who killed Custer? It will never be definitely known. The Indians themselves never agreed. Among those named by them as the slayer, were Two Moons and Harshay Horse of the Cheyennes; White Bull, nephew of Sitting Bull; and Spotted Calf, a Santee who had fled from Minnesota.

It may well have been a Cheyenne, for those Indians, before the battle, claimed Custer as *theirs* — they had a death feud with him because of the Washita massacre. Years afterward, in 1909, Brave Bear, a Cheyenne, was *designated* by a council of chiefs to bear the distinction of "having killed Custer." It was an honor, no more than that, nor was it claimed to mean that Brave Bear — though he was a great warrior — actually did the deed. He himself never claimed it. Nobody really knows who did fire the fatal shot.

One story, however, has been disproved — that Custer committed suicide. He did not do so. He fell on the field of battle, brave to the last. In spite of his errors in judgment and policy, he became after his death, because of the tremendous publicity the battle received, what he vainly sought to be before his death: a national hero.

Reno, Benteen, and their men were rescued from their bluffs two days later by the approaching column under Terry and Gibbon, for which Custer should have waited. The bodies of Custer's men were found and buried.

In Custer's immediate command, not one survived. The death total was 208 officers and men. In Reno's command, 57 officers and men were killed and 52 wounded. The total casualties, therefore, were 317. Bodies of 3 officers, a surgeon, and 2 enlisted men were never found. They may have been captured and tortured to death.

The Sioux had won their greatest victory. But the Battle of the Little Bighorn, in a sense, was their finish, for a very simple reason: after that conflict they never again had enough ammunition to fight a regular battle.

More troops came. The Sioux bands scattered and were relentlessly pursued. Sitting Bull shouted his defiance: "Almighty God made me an Indian — but not an Agency Indian!" But he was driven north across the border into Canada by Colonel Nelson A. Miles, and for a time found refuge there.

In late November Colonel Ranald S. McKenzie attacked and destroyed Dull Knife's Cheyenne village in arctic weather. A few days afterward, beaten and starving, the Cheyennes despairingly surrendered.

Not until January 8, 1877, was Crazy Horse finally defeated by Miles at Wolf Mountain — with the use of artillery, when the Sioux had scarcely any rifle bullets with which to shoot back. He surrendered late in April. When, the following September, he resisted an effort — contrary to all agreements — to put him in prison, he was bayonetted to death by a soldier.

Captain Bourke, one of those who fought hardest against him, wrote:

Crazy Horse was one of the great soldiers of his day and generation. As the grave of Custer marked the high water mark of Sioux supremacy in the trans-Mississippi region, so the grave of Crazy Horse marked the ebb.

Crazy Horse was to have been put behind bars — when he met his death — because he refused to lead and raise a company of Sioux scouts to fight against other Indians. For already a new war had broken out, and one of the most brilliant of all Indian leaders, Chief Joseph of the Nez Percés, was baffling and defeating column after column of soldiers in fierce battles and unbelievable marches far to the west of the Sioux country.

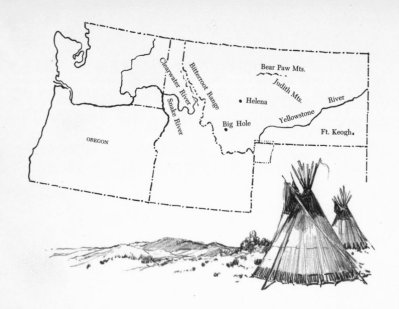

The map shows labels: Bear Paw Mts., Judith Mts., Helena, River, Bitterroot Range, Clearwater River, Snake River, Yellowstone, Big Hole, Ft. Keogh, OREGON

The Long, Long Trail | 7

FOR THE BEGINNINGS of this chapter in the Indian wars we must go back briefly to the year 1872. In a tepee beside beautiful Lake Wallowa, in northeast Oregon, a chief lay dying. His people, the Nez Percés, were frantic with grief and fear, for always he had been their wise guide in critical times, and now they were facing a life-and-death crisis.

For years the white men had coveted their Wallowa valley and used every pressure to make them cede the land and move to a reservation in northern Idaho. This their wise chief, known as Old Joseph, steadfastly refused to do. Who would counsel them now, when he was gone?

Before his last breath, the old chief called to his

bedside his eldest son, a tall young man, straight as an arrow and wonderfully handsome. He had a long Indian name, but he was destined to go down in history as Chief Joseph, taking his name from his father.

"My son," said the old chief, weakly but very earnestly, "give ear to me. When I am gone think of your country. You are the chief of these people. Always remember that your father never sold his country. A few more years and white men will be all around you. They have their eyes on this land. My son, never forget my dying words. This country holds your father's body. Never sell the bones of your father and mother."

Young Joseph walked forth from the death lodge, the chief of his people. His father's last words were his constant guide in the strange adventures and battle-filled days that followed. He was then twenty-four years old and little known, except as a handsome young man and a fine hunter. He had never seen a shot fired in anger. Yet such were his qualities that before he was through, he taught the best soldiers in the United States Army lessons in strategy and tactics.

What kind of people were the Nez Percés? Their name (in French signifying "Pierced Noses," from a long forgotten custom of wearing nose ornaments), was pronounced *nay per-say'* by the early French, but today whites and Indians always pronounce it *nez purses*. They had a long record of friendship to the white men, remaining peaceful in all the wars with the Modocs, Klamaths, Cayuses, Spokanes, Rogue River Indians, and other coastal tribes. It was their boast that no white man's blood had ever been shed by a Nez Percé, even though Nez Percés had died at white men's hands.

Yet the dealings of white men with the tribe were disgraceful. By treaty they had been guaranteed a large district in Idaho and the Wallowa valley of Oregon. In Idaho lived what were called the Upper Nez Percés. The Lower Nez Percés, of whom Joseph was chief, lived in Oregon.

Discovery of gold, and the usual inability of the

Chief Joseph

government to make its citizens obey its laws, resulted
in a new "treaty" — signed, it appears, only by the
Upper Nez Percés — whereby their brothers in Oregon
were to give up their lands and move into Idaho. This
was the treaty Old Joseph did not sign and refused
to recognize.

Now to return to the year 1877. In that year the
Sioux had at last been defeated, and General O. O.
Howard, commanding in Idaho, was told to round up
the Nez Percés and put them on the Fort Lapwai reservation.

He asked young Joseph and some of his subchiefs to
talk with him at Fort Lapwai. The general came off
second best in the debate. An example of Joseph's
shrewd reasoning was this answer to Howard's statement that the Wallowa country had been ceded by
treaty to the white man:

If we ever owned the country we own it still, for we
never sold it. Suppose a white man should come to me
and say, "Joseph, I like your horses, and I want to buy
them." I say to him, "No, my horses suit me, I will not
sell them." Then he goes to my neighbor and says to
him, "Joseph has some good horses. I want to buy them
but he refuses to sell." My neighbor answers, "Pay me
the money and I will sell you the horses." The white man
returns to me and says, "Joseph, I have bought your
horses, and you must let me have them." If we sold our

lands to the government, that was the only way they were bought.

Howard, a one-armed veteran, was a good friend of the Indians, and usually sympathized with their troubles. But this time he lost his temper and arrested Too-hul-hul-sote, a chief who argued too sharply with him. Joseph, with his other chiefs — his fiery younger brother Ollicot, White Bird, Hush-hush-cute, and Looking Glass — at once left the council.

The captive chief was released, but before further negotiations matters were taken out of Joseph's hands. Some time before, a rancher named Richard Divine had killed a Nez Percé called Eagle Blanket. While Joseph was away, three young braves rode out from the camp — then in White Bird Canyon, where it opens into the Snake River Gorge on the Idaho side — and slew Divine. Other reckless young Indians joined them, and eighteen white persons were killed along the Salmon River before they returned to the village.

Joseph had not planned such a thing, and was sorrowful when he heard of it. But his people were in a fighting mood. He must go with them or against them. He felt it was his duty to stay with his tribe.

General Howard knew he must punish the Indians. Under Colonel David Perry, about 100 cavalry rode for White Bird Canyon, reaching it June 17. Nobody expected much fighting, since the Nez Percés had always been peaceful. But they had not counted on Joseph.

His scouts discovered the troops miles away — as soon as they entered the deep gorge and rode down it looking for the Nez Percé village. The young chief had no war experience, but he took command in his first battle as if he were a veteran of a hundred engagements, and with his 200 warriors set a perfect trap.

As the cavalry advanced, the buttes ahead suddenly seemed alive with Indians, and with a clattering roll of rifle fire, a band of mounted Nez Percés, led by Ollicot charged the startled troopers. Back they fell, then wheeled into line to repel the attack. The Indians swirled away — it was a feint — and Joseph closed the other jaw of his trap.

About 100 of his warriors, led by White Bird, were hidden in the underbrush at one side of the canyon. Out they came, howling and shooting. The cavalry line crumpled, and the Nez Percés chased them all the way to Grangeville, fifteen miles away. In the stunning defeat an officer and 36 men were killed out of 100 who started the battle. The Nez Percé loss was slight, since the Indians fought largely from cover.

When the news reached Fort Lapwai, Howard marched with 300 men and three pieces of artillery.

But his foe had left White Bird Canyon. So entangled did the general become in the mountains that Joseph was able to cut two scouting forces to pieces, and retreat to the Clearwater River. There Looking Glass's band joined him, raising his force of braves to 250, and also increasing his noncombatant list. He now had 450 women, children, and aged to care for, besides baggage and 2000 horses. Nevertheless, he chose a battlefield and faced his enemy.

As Howard's scouts crept up to the Clearwater, the morning of July 11, shots crackled out. The Indians were there — behind rude breastworks on the opposite

side of the river.

Howard, who had been reinforced, brought up his main body of 580 men, and the firing became a steady and heavy roar. It was a battle the like of which the army had never fought with Indians. Here warriors fought from entrenchments, repelled bayonet charges, attacked positions held by soldiers, virtually besieged a command outnumbering them two to one.

With such skill did Joseph handle his warriors that he almost turned Howard's flank, and would have captured his supply train but for the arrival of additional troops.

Night came down black in the canyon. There were

occasional sputters of shots in the darkness. But next morning Howard's artillery — a howitzer and two Gatling guns — arrived, and Joseph fell back.

Holding Howard off with a handful of braves, Joseph retreated slowly. Forty soldiers were dead and wounded. The Nez Percé loss was heavier, chiefly because of the artillery fire. But Joseph had lost no honors.

When he reached Kamiah Falls, Idaho, Joseph made a decision. For his people's sake he decided to leave the country and seek safety elsewhere. How it cost him is shown by his own words:

I said in my heart that I would give up my country. I would give up my father's grave. I would give up everything rather than have the blood of my people on my hands . . . I love that land more than all the world. A man who would not love his father's grave is worse than a wild animal.

With a heavy heart, he began what was to be a terrible retreat of 2000 miles, with certainty of pursuit and hard fighting, in hope of reaching Canada and safety. His way was barred to the north, so he must go east, over the mountains, into Montana.

First there was the Lolo Pass over the Bitterroot Range, one of the most difficult trails in America, by which he must move his people. Its jagged rocks, fallen timber, narrow trails, dizzy abysses, steep and crooked climbs, were made worse because it rained almost every day, so that the ground was dangerously slippery. Horses fell over cliffs, baggage was lost, but wet and cold the people struggled on, day after day.

On the far side of the pass was a new fort. Joseph avoided it by turning south, along the Bitterroot Valley, to the Big Hole River, where he camped in a beautiful wooded spot. In this march the Indians did no damage. The white settlers were friendly, selling them necessaries. When later the military protested, these frontiersmen replied that the Nez Percés always had been good Indians and they saw no reason to fight them.

Such kindness, however, made the Indians believe the war was over. They camped peacefully, never dreaming that Colonel John Gibbon was coming at top speed from Helena, Montana, to intercept them.

At daybreak, August 9, a Nez Percé herdboy saw the soldiers fording the stream. He whooped a warning, but the troops charged through the camp, driving the Indians out into the bushes and trees beyond.

But Gibbon had caught something more than he planned. Back through the woods came the Nez Percés. The soldiers could hear their chiefs encouraging them. In a fierce charge, with hand-to-hand fighting, the troopers were driven out of the village. Indian sharpshooters picked off officers. Gibbon was wounded, but formed his men back to back and sent them charging in opposite directions through the trees — only to be repelled.

The situation grew desperate. Entrenching themselves on a knoll, the soldiers fought for their lives, while about them all day the Nez Percé rifles snarled and snapped. Learning that a howitzer was being brought up, Joseph sent thirty braves, who captured the gun, put it out of commission, and seized 2000 rounds of badly needed ammunition.

Night fell. The troops clung to their knoll, nearly dead of thirst although volunteers, covered by a firing party, managed to crawl to the river and fill a few canteens. Next morning the Nez Percés were gone.

Joseph had lost 89 dead, of whom 50 were women and children. But Gibbon's command was crippled, with 30 dead and 40 wounded, some mortally. He was very thankful next day to see the advance guards of Howard's force, which had followed the Indians over the Lolo Pass.

Now Joseph must retreat south. It was not the direction he wished to go, for his goal was Canada. Far back hung his peerless scouts, and through these he learned presently that Howard, leaving Gibbon, was following him. Joseph paused just long enough for a sharp night attack at Camas Meadows, cutting loose the soldiers' pack train and killing or wounding eight men. That stopped Howard, who could not pursue without more supplies.

Westward turned Joseph, through Yellowstone Park. There his braves surprised two parties of tourists. Some of the men, who resisted, were killed or wounded. Two women were captured, but were released unharmed.

Now at last Joseph could head north. Following Clark's Fork of the Yellowstone River out of the park, he fought a sharp rear-guard action, September 13, with the 7th Cavalry under Colonel Samuel D. Sturgis. There were only about 100 Nez Percés, but it took the 350 troopers and a band of Crow Indian scouts most of the day to drive the few braves out of their positions. The Crow scouts, however, succeeded in running off 900 of the Nez Percés' horses — a serious loss. Twenty-one Nez Percés were killed or wounded in the fight, while Sturgis lost 15 men. The cavalry remained where it was when the Nez Percés withdrew to continue the march.

Joseph now had left behind three forces of soldiers, each of which outnumbered him, but were crippled or exhausted. Slowed by the loss of their horses, the Nez Percés pushed north through the Judith Mountains, brushed aside a few soldiers at a crossing of the

Missouri River, and drove onward toward the Bear Paw Mountains.

It was an agonizing march, worn-out ponies dropping at every mile. Human flesh and blood could not stand it for ever. When they reached the Bear Paws, Joseph out of sheer humanity told his people to rest for a few days. He was only thirty miles from Canada, and seemed safe.

But he lacked the advantage of the white man's telegraph, and did not know of another peril approaching him. At that very time a new force, under Colonel Miles, with fresh troops, fresh horses, and fresh scouts, was hammering its way from Fort Keogh, Montana, to cut him off.

On a cold and stormy morning, September 30, 1877, Miles found the Indian camp, pitched on the north side of the mountains almost in sight of Canada. With the first shots, Joseph took in the situation with what must have been sickening despair. His few remaining horses were swept away, his enemy was outspread before him, he was outnumbered four to one. But he would fight to the last.

Keeping his 5th Infantry in reserve, Miles sent three of his five troops of cavalry charging across the cup-shaped ravine where the village lay. From cliffs overlooking it, a level sheet of flame from rifles began to cut them down. The Nez Percés were at bay at last, but they were going to make their end memorable.

Down went Captains Myles Moylan and Edward Godfrey, wounded. Half of Captain Owen Hale's men had fallen. Yet the troopers rode on. At the foot of the cliffs they dismounted and struggled on foot up through the boulders and underbrush. The men were wilting like autumn leaves, but still they fought upward.

Using toes, fingernails, almost teeth, they made the last grim climb. Twenty feet from the top, brave, chivalrous Captain Hale, joking in the face of danger, was killed. Only one officer was left, but the men climbed right into the heated Nez Percé rifle muzzles. It was madness — as brave a charge as American troops ever made. They did the impossible. The top of the bluff was reached: the cliffs were theirs.

But at what a cost! Of the 115 who began the charge, 53 lay dead or wounded down the slope. And meantime, like a master general, Joseph had withdrawn his braves at just the right minute, to a position higher in the mountains.

During this furious fighting a small part of the Nez Percé band, led by White Bird, and including Joseph's ten-year-old daughter, sifted through the troop line and eventually reached Sitting Bull's Sioux camp in Canada.

But in the Bear Paw Mountains the fight raged on.

Miles brought up his full regiment of infantry, the rest of his cavalry, and his two cannon. An infantry charge was beaten back by the deadly Nez Percé rifles, but Ollicot was killed — Joseph's younger brother, whose dash and ardor had turned many a critical situation. It seemed to take the life out of Joseph.

By nightfall Miles knew he could not carry the Indian position by direct assault. He took up besieging lines. All next day the artillery bombarded the Nez Percés, the shells bursting with shattering explosions among their rocks, so it seemed they must be wiped out. But when the soldiers cautiously advanced, they were fiercely driven back.

That evening Howard and a few aides rode into camp. His and Sturgis' weary forces were coming up to reinforce Miles. Next morning, October 1, a white flag fluttered in the Indian lines. With relief Miles saw it, for he had lost a fifth of his men, and dreaded the possibility that Sitting Bull and his Sioux might come down from Canada on his rear.

Sunset came, and Joseph, with five of his chiefs, met Miles, Howard, and some officers on a little hill between the lines. The great Nez Percé handed Miles his rifle, butt first, in sign of surrender. Then he spoke a few beautiful, pathetic sentences, ending, "Hear me, my chiefs! My heart is sick and sad. From where the sun now stands, I will fight no more, forever!"

It was the end of a campaign almost without parallel. Joseph, who never had more than 300 warriors, was opposed by 5000 soldiers and hundreds of armed civilians and Indian scouts. In sixteen battles he actually met 2000 troops. Of these he killed or wounded 266. His own loss in killed and wounded (including women and children) was 239. Again and again he defeated the best soldiers in the nation; marched 2000 miles through enemy country without a supply train and carrying his noncombatants; and came within thirty miles of his goal, in spite of every handicap.

The captured Nez Percés — 87 warriors and 254 women and children — were sent to the Indian Territory, but later returned to reservations near their former home, where they now live peacefully. Joseph, in 1903, was an honored guest of President Theodore Roosevelt and General Miles in Washington. He died in 1904, at Nespelm, Washington, admired and respected alike by red men and white.

Yet with the end of the Nez Percé War, there was no rest for the hard-working frontier army. Far to the south, in the sun-blasted deserts of Arizona and New Mexico, there was a continuing, ruthless, deadly war, with a people far different from the chivalrous Nez Percés — the dread Apaches, who very soon were to test the courage and endurance of the soldiers to the utmost.

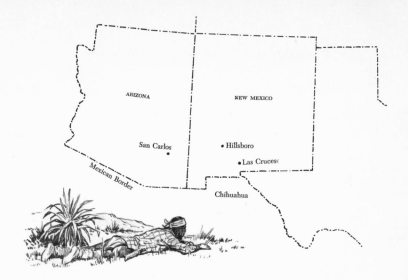

The Hunting of the Apaches | 8

ON A HEATED DAY late in August, 1879, a band of dark-faced savages squatted on a height just south of the line between Mexico and the United States, staring northward. They were Apaches, the deadliest, most elusive, and maddening Indian enemies the American army ever faced.

Their country was a wilderness — a vast desert and a fearful one, with but few small settlements and oases. Perhaps no more dreadful campaigning ground ever existed, yet the Apaches knew every foot of it, every spring and water pocket, every trail and hideout.

From the very ferocity of their surroundings — the burned-out valleys and plains, the inhospitable and unkempt peaks — the Apaches had gained a ferocity of their own. Lean, sun-baked, and filled with shocking vitality and cruelty, they were ruthless in warfare. They slaughtered women and children as quickly as men, and sometimes tortured captives fiendishly. For this reason the Apaches were hated as few Indians ever were. They returned that hate, for they, too, had been massacred and abused in the more than twenty years since their great chief Mangas Coloradas was murdered. So it became a vicious circle, each new act adding bitterness to the enmity between red men and white.

To recount all their movements, raids, ambushes, and fights would be impossible in this book. But we can follow the deadly and snake-like movements of the greatest of all their raiders, Victorio, as an illustration and example of all the rest.

Before the squatting warriors on the height that August day, stood Victorio, a compactly built man, nearly sixty years old, about five feet ten inches tall, deep-throated, broad-chested, his legs slightly bowed. His face set him apart from the others — a face fierce and wild, very wide through the cheekbones, with a grim mouth, strong nose and jaw, and eyes as hard as glittering bits of flint.

After Mangas Coloradas no leader had arisen who could rally the Apaches as a people. They fought in separate bands, each with its own chief. Cochise, of

the Chiricahuas, had done some fighting and plundering. The same could be said of the Mescalero, White Mountain, and Tonto Apaches. But they all surrendered sooner or later. Even Victorio consented to go on a reservation — for a time.

But when they told him he must move from his home at Warm Springs, New Mexico, to San Carlos, a heated Arizona basin, in order to make room for white gold miners and ranchers, he rebelled and fled to Old Mexico. Now he stood before his braves, looking northward. Those mauve-tinted mountains on the horizon marked the international border. Come nightfall, and a daring venture would begin. With fewer

than 100 warriors, Victorio was to invade the United
States — then a nation of 60,000,000 people!

He had no hope of driving the white men out of his
ancestral lands. They swarmed too thickly for that.
But *this* Victorio did intend to do: slay as many and
do as much damage as he could, in a vengeful raid.
And after that, escape — if he was lucky — back into
Mexico.

With not an eye to witness their silent entry, Victorio's warriors rode over the border that night. The
first notice that they were in the United States was a
message of blood.

At Warm Springs, in the old Mimbreño country, a
company of the 9th Cavalry under Captain Ambrose
E. Hooker was camped the night of September 4. Suddenly the darkness was lit by vivid flashes of rifle fire,
and the angry clatter of reports brought the sleeping
troopers to their feet. With wild yells sounding high
above the thunder of stampeding hoofs, the Apaches
were gone. Eight troopers lay dead; Victorio had captured all the company's horses without losing a brave.

So began Victorio's War. In the next two years his
Apaches left a mocking trail a thousand miles long
for the army to follow, back and forth across Arizona,
New Mexico, western Texas, and northern Old Mexico.
All the way it was marked by burned ranches, cap-

tured wagons and stages, and bodies of victims, some showing evidence of cruelties that made the pursuing soldiers go white with rage.

The fighting was haphazard. Riding along a washout, a file of troopers might hear the spiteful reports of rifles, and some saddles would be emptied. Before they could locate their foes and get into action, only the flutter of the last dusty breechclouts of the hostiles could be seen, so high up among the rocks that there was no chance to catch them.

Sometimes, of course, there was a real fight. Then the carbines cracked eagerly, bullets glanced from rocks and went screaming off like lost souls across the landscape, and now and then a swarthy brave fell stricken among the cactus and rocks. But for the most part Apache encounters were a sudden ambush, a hurried recovery of the soldiers, and a wary retreat by the savages, with nothing gained for the troops, and some good men lost.

After the swoop on Hooker, the alarm went out. Every troop command in New Mexico began groping frantically through the desert, but for a time Victorio and his braves seemed to disappear into the thin air. Then, ten days later, the chief struck again, suddenly and savagely.

A posse of ranchers and miners went "Indian hunting." They found an Indian trail near Hillsboro, New

Mexico, and shortly after found Victorio — to their sorrow, for he turned on them with snarling fury. Ten of them were killed and all their horses captured by the raiders.

For a time Victorio hid in the Mimbres Mountains. There he was joined by furtive braves, who had stolen away from their reservations and by some underground information knew his hiding place, until he mustered about 140 warriors.

On September 18, Lieutenant Colonel N. A. M. Dudley located the hostiles in the rugged canyons at the head of Las Animas Creek. Victorio had posted his desert wolves in almost impregnable positions among the rocks, but the Apaches were badly outnumbered

by Dudley's four companies of soldiers, and his scouts.
The first sharp rifle shots sounded. Then, throughout
the day, the uproar of battle echoed through the
mountains and canyons.

For the troops it was most perilous and difficult
fighting — from rock to rock and bush to bush, without
water, under the beating sun. Deadly as so many
rattlesnakes, the Apaches fought, each in his chosen
spot, behind a clump of growth, or a rock, where only
the smoke of his rifle betrayed his presence.

When night fell Dudley counted his losses. Five
soldiers, 2 Navajo scouts, and 1 white scout were dead,
a number were wounded, and 38 horses were killed
or crippled. The soldiers, who had not been able to

see an enemy to get their sights on all day, did not know of a single Indian they had killed. It was clear that Victorio was too strong to be dislodged, so in the darkness Dudley withdrew, carrying his dead and wounded.

By now Victorio had fought and beaten the white men three times, killed 26 of them, wounded many others, captured a large number of horses, picked up much booty, and recruited some good warriors from the reservations. So he headed back to Mexico.

But the border was swarming with troops. Near Warm Springs, Major A. P. Morrow, with 198 officers and men, struck the retreating Apaches and pursued them for two days in a running fight, killing three Indians.

Victorio shook him off, but Morrow followed across the international boundary. He lost two men killed and two wounded, and only succeeded in capturing an empty camp. He and his soldiers, without water for three days and nights, and almost at the limit of their endurance, staggered back across the border to Fort Bayard, New Mexico, November 3.

Victorio had an understanding with the small Mexican ranchers and sheepherders, for he wanted to use Mexico as a base, knowing perfectly the advantage of playing back and forth across the international line.

The people south of the border knew they would be allowed to live just so long as they furnished him with arms, food, horses, and ammunition.

So when the grim brown warriors with their steel-trap mouths rode up to the little adobe *casas* (houses), the owners came forth with anything that was demanded, and were glad to get off with their lives. They even sold rifles to the Apaches. How can one blame them? It was that — or die.

North of the border, settlers and soldiers were rejoicing at being rid of the Indians when, one afternoon, the stagecoach from Fort Davis dashed into Fort Quitman with the driver and one passenger dead and arrows still quivering in the woodwork of its sides. That was in March, 1880. Soon telegraph wires were cut between Fort Quitman and Eagle Springs.

Victorio was back! Somehow he had eluded the troops who literally plastered the border. At once the usual reports of Apache horrors began to come in — cowboys, prospectors, lone travelers killed here and there, ranches burned, stock stolen, as the Indians left a smoking, bloody swath across the Texas Big Bend country.

By April 8, Victorio was in the San Andreas Mountains, in New Mexico, where he could almost look down on the streets of Las Cruces. There, Colonel Edward Hatch, with the 9th Cavalry, tried conclusions with him. But Dudley's experience was repeated — the Apaches killed or wounded eight of their enemies, lost only three themselves, and shot so many of the troop horses that it was impossible to follow when they decided to withdraw.

Next — as the death toll showed — Victorio was back in Texas. Colonel B. H. Grierson, camped at Eagle Springs with almost 1000 men, believed the hostiles were headed for the isolated Fresno Springs. Reaching there by a forced march, he posted his soldiers about the springs, so that when the Indians arrived, they could be surrounded and killed.

About noon next day the first Apache riders appeared. Then the soldiers almost held their breath as the main body — more than 100 warriors — came into view. It was Victorio's band without a doubt, and it looked as though the old wolf had reached his end at last.

But before the Apaches were in the net, a wagon train appeared, crawling slowly toward the springs. Instantly the Indians took cover, and the hidden soldiers watched helplessly the unfolding of an ambush within an ambush, as Victorio, wholly unaware of the near presence of the troops, prepared to overwhelm the train.

As the minutes passed it grew apparent that unless Grierson saved them the wagon men who had blun-

dered into the scene would be massacred. Angry and disappointed, he sent his men to the rescue of the teamsters.

The astonished Apaches, for the first time seeing how near to disaster they had been, rode hard to escape, losing two or three warriors, but at last leaving Grierson behind. Thereafter, to quote a military report, this campaign "resolved itself into a chase of the hostiles from one range of mountains to another, with frequent skirmishes, but no decisive fights."

Though some 5000 soldiers were trying to find Victorio, he eluded them and on August 11 was once more across the border into Mexico.

His truce with the small ranchers and herders in Mexico did not extend to the large ranches and mines. Moving slowly south through Chihuahua, he swept those places clean. Such an outcry was raised by big landowners that the Mexican government put forces in the field to halt the Apaches.

Victorio did not stop, however, until he reached the Candelaria Mountains, deep in Mexico. There he camped among nearly inaccessible peaks, while his scouts from towering lookouts watched in all directions.

At Carrizal, the nearest town, it was reported that Indians were in the Candelarias; but it was supposed to be a small band — perhaps no more than five or six *bronco* (outlaw) Apaches. Had the citizens known how powerful the band was in truth, and that it was led by Victorio himself, the twin tragedies that followed would not have occurred.

Not knowing, however, Don José Rodríguez, with other large landowners who had suffered from raids, on November 6 formed a party of fifteen men and set forth to find, and if possible destroy, the hostiles.

Their approach was seen by the Apaches on November 7. It was a situation very much to Victorio's liking. Calling forty or fifty of his braves, he laid as clever an ambush as an Indian ever devised; an ambush that was a psychological as well as a military masterpiece.

As the Mexicans rode through a deep canyon between two peaks, a sudden spray of bullets from cliffs to the north greeted them. To the south were some inviting boulders which appeared to offer excellent shelter. There the party took refuge.

It was exactly what Victorio had planned. He had not placed any warriors among those rocks, but had put them higher — converting the inviting boulders into a death trap worthy of his sinister intelligence.

When Rodríguez and his men threw themselves behind this "shelter," grim Apaches were watching them from above and behind. The Mexicans were at their mercy. A signal shot — and the slaughter began. There was no escape and no protection. Every man of the posse was slain.

But Victorio was not through. When, in due time, Rodríguez and his party did not return to Carrizal, a second posse of fourteen men set out to learn what had happened to their friends.

They probably counted on the fact that Apaches seldom lingered long at the scene of a fight, but they did not know Victorio. Here it was that his supreme cunning revealed itself. His first ambuscade was clever enough, but never before had it occurred to an Indian leader to use the victims of one trap as bait to entrap a second party.

Not a hostile was in sight when the rescuers from Carrizal arrived. The bodies of the Rodríguez party were found. Their sorrowing friends began to gather them to a central burying place, not dreaming that almost above their heads fierce eyes were fixed on them, and death awaited.

When the fourteen living Mexicans were grouped about their slain kinsmen, the signal was given. Shooting did not last long. Too openly exposed were the Mexicans, too numerous and well posted the Apaches. Never again did Carrizal see the faces of her sons.

Thereafter, Victorio entered Texas again. Never was he inactive. Twisting back and forth through the Big Bend country, he raided in New Mexico, before returning across the border. Texas Rangers and American cavalry now followed him down into Mexico.

Hunted like a mad wolf across the ranges and deserts, Victorio pushed southward. He sent two parties of braves, one to go north again, the other to raid through Mexico, then made his leisurely way, with frequent halts, toward a refuge he knew in the Tres Castillos Mountains of Chihuahua.

Behind, American fighters were pushing him. Mexican troops were in front. It was the Mexicans who intercepted Victorio.

A deep basin in the Tres Castillos, which could be

entered only through a box canyon, was a favorite Apache camping ground. Colonel Joaquín Terrazas, with a strong force of Mexican soldiers and Tarahumari Indian scouts, reached this basin before Victorio, and posted his men in places of vantage about it, every foot of it covered by their rifles.

With most of his best warriors away on raids, Victorio led his people, largely women and children, through the box canyon and into the pleasant valley beyond, without fear or hesitation.

And now he, who had ambushed so many, was himself trapped. All at once the rocks echoed with a deafening roar of rifle fire, and Apaches died by scores in the sleet of lead. Ringed about by his enemy, but never more dangerous than when cornered, Victorio gathered his few remaining braves, and fought back, killing many.

Night fell, but still the guns flamed and spat through the dark hours. By daybreak the Apaches were out of ammunition. The Mexicans charged.

There Victorio died, rallying his few braves for a hand-to-hand fight. He was killed instantly, in the heat of battle, as he would have wished. He was sixty years old at his death, an implacable and cruel enemy, but his long fight against hopeless odds was inspired by something akin to patriotism.

Of him, Ralph Emerson Twitchell, the New Mexico

historian, wrote:

> He outwitted two generals of the American army and
> one in command of the Mexican forces. He captured from
> the governor of Chihuahua in one campaign, over 500
> horses. He and his warriors killed over 200 New Mexi-
> cans (and many Texans), more than 100 soldiers, and 200
> citizens of the Mexican republic . . . This was the result
> of the greed of the settler, and the corrupt policy . . .
> of the management of Indian affairs in the Southwest.
> If Victorio had been permitted to remain at Ojo Caliente
> [Warm Springs, New Mexico] it is more than likely that
> the terrible devastation . . . would never have occurred.

The Apaches never had another leader of Victorio's
military ability. Nana, a subchief almost eighty years
old, led one memorable raid into New Mexico, but he
was too old to command another foray.

Other chiefs were blunderers by comparison. Loco,
for example, tried to escape from the San Carlos res-
ervation in April, 1882. He was defeated at Stein's
Peak, New Mexico, by Lieutenant Colonel G. A.
Forsyth (the same who fought the Cheyennes on the
Arikaree River). Later he fell into an ambush of
Mexican troops in which his band was all but ex-
terminated.

Equally brief and unfortunate, for them, was an
outbreak by the White Mountain Apaches in July,

1882. Three of their braves were hanged at Fort Apache, Arizona, for an attack on troops who arrested — and killed — a tribal medicine man. At that, 54 braves, led by Nan-tia-tish, swept through the San Carlos Valley, raiding ranches and killing 18 persons. But they were soundly beaten in the deep gorge of Canyon Diablo (near Winslow, Arizona) and the survivors crept back to their reservation.

Chato and Ulzana each made a short raid north from Mexico. And Geronimo obtained a lot of undeserved publicity as the last "great" Apache war chief. Actually, Geronimo never was a chief at all. He was in reality an outlaw, against whom even his own people turned. Crook called him "the human tiger," and Miles referred to him as "the worst Indian that ever lived." He was cunning, bloodthirsty, a great talker, and a great liar.

He spent his time in Mexico, where he could prey on the poor villagers and small herders — the very people Victorio spared. United States forces pursued him down there, with Mexico's willing permission, in an effort to rid that country of him, and get him back on the reservation. And his long escape from capture was due chiefly to the smallness of his band, which at times numbered less than thirty braves. As Charles F. Lummis wrote:

The difficulty of cornering a dozen or fifty supremely elusive foes in a territory as big as Europe, is palpable. Were there ten thousand Apaches on the war path, the task of hunting them down would be simple; but beside the catching of that handful, the proverbial needle in a haystack is a sinecure of discovery.

Twice Geronimo surrendered and promised to keep the peace; and twice he broke away, to murder, torture, and rob with his small band of outlaw Apaches.

In the end it was Apaches — Chiricahuas of his own tribe — who ran him down. About 300 of them enlisted as scouts, and these, in companies headed by picked officers — men like Captains H. W. Lawton and Charles B. Gatewood, and the gallant Captain Emmett Crawford, who was killed by Mexican irregulars — kept up a never-ending pursuit, trailed him time and again deep into Mexico, and followed him so relentlessly that at length he gave up, for good.

Geronimo and his band were sent to Florida. Later they were taken to Oklahoma, where Geronimo died in 1909. Finally the rest of the band were returned to the Mescalero reservation in New Mexico to live.

And here is an interesting footnote: the last Apache "war" of history was fought against *one man!*

When the Geronimo prisoners were transported across the continent, one of them, a warrior named Massai (pronounced *mah-say*) escaped from the train somewhere east of St. Louis. Nobody but an Apache could have equaled what he then did. Alone, in a thickly settled section, without food or weapons, without a map and with only his unerring homing instinct to guide him, he made his way across half the continent to his home land in Arizona, *without ever being seen by a human eye.*

There he began a one-man war, against both the

United States and Mexico. He bushwhacked and out-guessed soldiers, scouts, and civilians back and forth across the border for about three years. He won his war, too, for they never kept him from going where he wanted, or doing what he wished, and he killed a great many more of them than they did of him — perhaps 100 persons all told, according to one estimate.

He finally disappeared, about 1889 or 1890, and it was reported that he was killed in Mexico. But old Apaches on the White Mountain reservation will tell you today that Massai was never slain by Mexican soldiers. They will say that he joined and lived with one of the *bronco* Apache bands in the Mexican mountains — whose descendants, incidentally, still live there, as wild as of old, and sometimes communicate secretly with the reservation Apaches in the United States even today.

Whatever the truth of this, Massai ceased his raiding. So peace came at last to the desert.

But not to the northern plains. About the time the last fighting Apache disappeared from the ken of the white man, a new, great trouble was building like an ominous cloud in the Dakotas, a blood-red cloud which would bring a strange, belated hour of fire, fury, and death to white men and red men in the land of the once mighty Sioux.

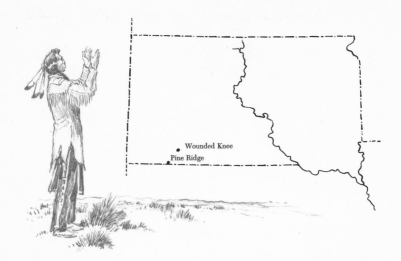

Wounded Knee
Pine Ridge

The War with the Ghost Dancers | 9

IN THE WINTER OF 1889 the plains tribes were seized with the fervor of a strange religion. The Sioux, in particular, heard of an Indian messiah in the far West, and sent trusted warriors, led by Kicking Bear and Short Bull, to the distant country of the Paiutes, where the messiah's camp was reported to be, near Walker Lake, Nevada.

There the Sioux messengers saw the heralded "messiah." He was a full-blooded Paiute, about thirty-five years old, wearing white men's clothing, and tattooed on both wrists. His name was Wovoka (the Cutter), but in his youth he had lived with a white family named Wilson, so he was known to the whites as Jack Wilson. He spoke only Paiute and a little English, but he was able to converse, partly through interpreters, with his visitors.

Perhaps it was from his white associates that Wovoka conceived his weird half-Christian, half-pagan doctrine. To the Sioux messengers he said that some time before, when the sun "died" (an eclipse), he went into a trance and was taken to another world. There he saw God; and received a revelation, including rites to be practiced and a sacred dance which he was commanded to give to his people.

He proclaimed to his visitors that he was the Indian messiah, come to save the red men, and announced that he would soon move eastward, at which time vast herds of wild horses, buffalo, and deer would be driven before him, and dead Indians would rise and join the living. Then he taught them the sacred dance and other rites, and bade them go and herald his coming.

The excitement with which this was received by the Sioux when their messengers returned, was tremendous. Once before, they told each other, the messiah had come to save the white man, but the white man had not believed in him and killed him. Now he would save his red children! Conquered, despairing, often hungry, they hoped now for freedom and divine assistance in returning to the old, beloved way of life.

Other tribes received the same "revelation," and believed it with the same pathetic eagerness. Night by night, day by day, the drums beat in every Indian camp in Montana, Wyoming, Nebraska, the Dakotas, Texas, and Oklahoma, as the devotees continued in the sacred dance, which came to be known as the "Ghost Dance," so strenuously that many fell exhausted and some even died. A peculiar dress was worn by the dancers, the "ghost shirt."

For months the messiah craze was merely a religious mania. But a greenhorn Indian agent, R. F. Royer, at Pine Ridge, South Dakota, furnished the spark that turned it into an explosion. Newly appointed, and alarmed by the growing craze, he wired for troops. Soldiers arrived at Pine Ridge, October 19, 1890. At once thousands of Sioux took to the Dakota badlands.

Far north of Pine Ridge, on the Standing Rock reservation, lived Sitting Bull. The chief had consented in 1881 to return to the United States from Canada, and he was still the most influential living Sioux. He was quietly staying in his home, but wild rumors — with little foundation — named him as the "high priest" of the Ghost Dance religion.

By December a chief named Big Foot had gathered more than 2000 Indians in his camp east of Pine Ridge, and there were other camps inhabited by Ghost Dancers. General Nelson A. Miles, commanding the department, had to do something. He decided to arrest Sitting Bull and disarm the rest of the Indians.

The excuse came when, December 12, Sitting Bull asked for a pass to go from Standing Rock to Pine Ridge. It may have been a perfectly innocent request, but Major William McLaughlin, agent at Standing Rock, who feared the chief, was convinced that he meant to join the "hostiles" — so called, though they had not as yet committed one hostile act.

At Standing Rock, as on most reservations, a company of Indian police had been enlisted and trained. It was a body of men, as was strikingly usual with Indian scouts and police who swore to uphold the government, that was completely loyal and could be trusted to obey orders. To his Indian police McLaughlin gave the duty of arresting Sitting Bull.

In the dead of night, December 15, 1890, the police, led by Lieutenant Bull Head, and Sergeants Shave Head and Red Tomahawk, and backed by 100 soldiers with a Hotchkiss gun (a small, semiautomatic cannon), entered the Hunkpapa camp on the Grand River and surrounded Sitting Bull's cabin.

The chief was asleep on the floor when the Indian police entered before dawn, aroused him, and told him to dress and come with them. Dazed, then furious, he was hustled out of his home like a common criminal. Outside, his people had heard the commotion, and were gathering to see what was happening. At his appearance with the police, they began milling around the cabin, excitedly yelling taunts and abuse, with rifles very much in evidence.

All at once Sitting Bull balked.

"I am not going!" he shouted, his eyes blazing with anger at this insult. Then, in a loud voice, he began giving directions for his own rescue.

Out rang a sudden war whoop, followed by a shot.

Instantly other rifles began to crack.

Bull Head, leader of the Indian police, fell dying, shot by one of Sitting Bull's warriors. But as he fell, he pumped a bullet into the prisoner's body. An instant later, Red Tomahawk also shot the chief, and Sitting Bull pitched to the ground, dead.

With shots blazing all about them in the early dawn half-light, the Indian police fought bravely, doing their duty — even against their own kinsmen. Several were down, but the rest somehow beat off the furious Hunkpapas and crowded into the only shelter they could find, Sitting Bull's own cabin. There they found one of the chief's sons, Crowfoot, and killed him.

At the burst of rifle fire, Captain E. G. Fechet, commanding the troops, galloped up with his men. Carbines rang out, and the Hotchkiss gun went into action. As its shells sprayed among them, the Sioux scattered and angrily retreated across the river.

The soldiers and surviving police retreated to Standing Rock. Six police were dead or dying, and two were wounded. Eight Hunkpapa warriors were dead.

And there was Sitting Bull — once a figure of almost epic savage splendor, a legend while yet in his lifetime, and to his death a leader who thought of and for his people — killed, like King Philip and Pontiac before him, by members of his own race.

At news of Sitting Bull's death every Sioux reservation grew tense. Two skirmishes occurred near Big Foot's village on the Cheyenne River. But already the more levelheaded Indian leaders saw that it would be suicide to resist the army, and persuaded most of their people to return to their Agencies and give up their arms.

Among those who remained out was Big Foot's band, which was greatly reduced in numbers when hundreds of its people surrendered, December 21. Some angry refugees from Sitting Bull's camp had joined it, yet all might have gone in peaceably, had not an order come to arrest Big Foot himself. The night of December 22, he and his band fled again.

But 2000 troops were searching for Big Foot and it was only a question of time until they found him. Major S. M. Whiteside, with a battalion of the 7th Cavalry, located the village on Wounded Knee Creek, December 28, and ordered the Sioux to surrender.

"We want peace," Big Foot began. "I am sick and my people — "

"We will not parley with you," said Whiteside. "Surrender or fight!"

"We surrender," answered Big Foot. And then he added, showing the perplexity and despair of his people, "We would have done it before, if we had known where to find you."

His band numbered only 108 warriors and about 250 women and children, the rest having all gone in to the reservation. That evening these Indians were marched down the creek to the camp of the 7th Cavalry, and told to pitch their tepees near the soldiers. Big Foot had spoken the truth about being sick. In his tent that night he lay suffering from pneumonia.

Next morning, December 29, Colonel J. W. Forsyth formed the 500 men of the 7th Cavalry around the Indian village, trained four Hotchkiss guns on the prisoners, and ordered them disarmed. Into the lodges strode squads of soldiers, shouldering their way in, driving out the families, overturning beds and other

camp furniture, searching for weapons. Only a few guns were found, and the troopers believed the Indians were hiding them.

Meantime, the anger of the watching braves mounted at the rough and rude invasion of their homes. All at once Yellow Bird, a medicine man, began shouting to the Indians that the ghost shirts nearly all of them wore would stop the white men's bullets, and that they should resist. A soldier jerked at a brave's blanket, to see if a rifle was hidden beneath, and Yellow Bird tossed a handful of dust in the air.

Out rang a shot — an Indian's. In an instant the soldiers began to kill.

Later, the Indians charged that the 7th Cavalry had an old grudge against the Sioux for the Custer defeat at the Little Bighorn, which was why they ruthlessly massacred men, women, and children in the scenes that followed. But J. W. Mooney, who investigated the affair, wrote:

In justice to a brave regiment it must be said that a number of the men were new recruits . . . who had never before been under fire, were not yet imbued with military discipline, and were probably unable in the confusion to distinguish between men and women by their dress.

Whatever the truth of this, the soldiers now showed no mercy. In their first shattering volley about half of Big Foot's warriors were killed or wounded. Yet, like panthers, the survivors — perhaps fifty or sixty braves — sprang at the cordon that surrounded them. They were outnumbered ten to one, and many had no guns, but they seized knives, clubs, anything, and charged with desperate, hopeless bravery. Women, even children, took part. As an instance, Captain George B. Wallace fell wounded, and instantly was clubbed to death by an angry swarm of squaws.

Then the shells from the Hotchkiss guns began bursting among the Indians with terrible execution. Quickly the ground was covered with the dead and maimed. A few of the Sioux broke through and fled down a deep ravine, pursued by soldiers. Later bodies of women and children were found two or three miles away, where they had been overtaken and killed. General Miles afterward brought charges against Forsyth for his conduct, mentioning the murder of noncombatants at long distances from the fight. But Forsyth was exonerated, for he really tried to avert the massacre.

By nine o'clock the killing was over. Thirty-five soldiers and an Indian scout were killed or died of wounds later, and about as many were wounded. The full Indian loss will never be known. That night a blizzard set in and it was three days before the soldiers returned from Pine Ridge, where they took their wounded and prisoners. In the intense cold many wounded Indians, who might otherwise have recovered, froze to death.

Relatives braved the storm, sought out some of the bodies, and took them away for burial according to Sioux custom. General Miles reported not less than 200 Indians of both sexes and all ages were killed. But Mooney said that the whole number who were killed or died of exposure was very nearly 300. Fifty-one were brought in as prisoners. Hardly any of the 356 members of the band escaped. Among the dead was Big Foot, who was found lying shot and frozen in front of his tent.

At Pine Ridge, only nine miles from Wounded Knee, the Indians could hear the uproar of guns, and excitement was intense. Some leaped on horses to ride to the scene, but were forced back by the troops.

On a ridge west of the Agency a body of Brulé Sioux suddenly appeared. The faithful Indian police took positions behind a fence by the Agency school and fought a long range rifle engagement with those warriors on the heights. Presently the Brulés disappeared.

In the succeeding days several skirmishes took place, and once Forsyth was almost trapped, being

General Miles

saved by the arrival of the 9th Cavalry. But reinforcements kept arriving, until Miles had on hand 8000
troops — the largest force ever assembled in one place
to fight Indians.

Honestly horrified by Wounded Knee, Miles strove
day and night to prevent another explosion, which
would only mean more death and misery, without doing any good for either whites or Indians. Yet the out-
look was grave. Of the 25,000 Sioux on the northern
reservations, 21,500 were living in peace, and only
about 3500 — of whom perhaps 1000 were warriors
— were out. But others might join them at any minute. Night after night fires twinkled on the higher

buttes, and throughout the days puffs of smoke dotted the distant air — Indians signaling to each other.

It was wise counsel among the Sioux themselves that saved the situation. Leaders pointed out that the miraculous powers claimed by the messiah priests, who had promised immunity from death, were false. They closely estimated the number of troops arrayed against them and showed how futile it would be to fight such an overwhelming force.

Skirmishing continued, with a few more killed on each side, but gradually Miles's soldiers rounded up the rebellious Sioux, and began moving them toward Pine Ridge. Sullenly and grudgingly the Indians re-treated. Any moment — any unlucky incident — might bring on a general battle. For two days and nights Miles scarcely slept. But luck was with him — there were no incidents.

Then, all at once, in sight of the Agency, the Sioux refused to go any farther. That night, with double guards walking the army lines, Miles and his staff anxiously watched the flickering Indian campfires.

Slowly the moon rose. Suddenly furious shooting and yelling were heard in the Sioux camp. Believing the long-expected battle had come at last, the soldiers leaped to their arms. But nothing happened. The shooting and yelling died down. Dawn came quietly and peacefully.

Next morning the strange occurrence was explained. It was the last raging, heartsick outburst of the Sioux. Wild with their pent-up feelings, knowing they were helpless, they rushed out and shot down their own horses and dogs to give vent to their despairing rage.

After that the Indians marched peacefully into the Agency and camped. Thirty years of war with the Sioux had ended.

Wovoka, the "Indian messiah," died on October 4, 1932, in his squalid hut at Walker Lake, Nevada. The passing of the man once worshiped as almost divine by fanatical thousands was hardly noticed. It only recalled a troubled day in the West — the final, tragic stand of the red man.

Today the West is still the West, unparalleled in its wild grandeur, but many things have changed since the Ghost Dance War. The Indian has ceased retreating, and is coming back.

Gone are the teeming buffalo herds, but white-faced cattle now produce more meat than ever did the bison. And in the livestock industry Indians are important in the West. They are natural cowboys, who love the hard riding, danger, and hard work of that wild calling. Many tribes are turning to the raising of cattle, horses, sheep, and other livestock as a natural and even pleasurable occupation. As one example, the

once sullen Apac
blood cattle, whic
themselves.

By governmen
served, and India
many places. In
— and protected

Medicine has
far better than it
1928, when for t
deaths. Then the
in the United S
Now there are p
say they will nu

True, old "lon
ways — but thei
every modern ac
erations are bei
the surprises ha
skilled workers.
was built with
some of its most
wiring, and In
spected wherev
jects or in priv

In the admir
bulk large. Be

once sullen Apaches now own great herds of pure-blood cattle, which they handle, breed, and market for themselves.

By government aid Indian lands are being conserved, and Indian farms brought into productivity in many places. Indian arts and crafts are encouraged — and protected from sharpsters.

Medicine has done wonders, and Indian health is far better than it ever was. A turning point came about 1928, when for the first time Indian births exceeded deaths. Then there were only about 225,000 red men in the United States, and the number was falling. Now there are perhaps 400,000, and census estimates say they will number 700,000 by 1980.

True, old "long-hair" Indians take slowly to the new ways — but their eagerness to have their youth receive every modern advantage is notable. So the newer generations are being schooled and trained, and one of the surprises has been how quickly Indians become skilled workers. One of the great western power dams was built with 93 per cent Indian labor, including some of its most technical features such as the electric wiring, and Indian workers are being used and respected wherever they are available, on public projects or in private enterprise.

In the administration of their own affairs, Indians bulk large. Between 4000 and 6000 educated In-